ABD-RU-SHIN

IN THE LIGHT OF TRUTH · THE GRAIL MESSAGE

I

ABD-RU-SHIN

IN THE LIGHT
OF TRUTH

THE GRAIL MESSAGE

I

STIFTUNG GRALSBOTSCHAFT PUBLISHING CO.
STUTTGART

This book "In the Light of Truth", The Grail Message, by Abd-ru-shin, contains the translation according to the sense of the original German text. In the translation the expressions and sentences used by Abd-ru-shin to mediate the Living Word to the human spirit can only be rendered approximately. The reader should therefore realise that this translation cannot replace the original. However, if he makes the effort — as is desired by the Author — to absorb the contents intuitively, he will recognise the significance of this work for mankind, despite the deficiencies arising out of a translation.

Abd-ru-shin "In the Light of Truth", The Grail Message. Paperback edition, Volume I, Twenty-first edition 2016. Only Authorized edition. Title of the original German edition: „Im Lichte der Wahrheit" Gralsbotschaft. Owner of the copyrights Stiftung Gralsbotschaft, Stuttgart, Germany.

Printed in Germany by CPI books GmbH, Leck
ISBN: 978-3-87860-232-3

FREE YOURSELF FROM ALL DARKNESS!

HE WHO

MAKES NO EFFORT TO

GRASP THE WORD OF THE LORD

ARIGHT BURDENS HIMSELF

WITH GUILT!

FOR YOUR GUIDANCE!

THE BANDAGE falls, and belief becomes conviction. Liberation and redemption lie only in conviction!

I am addressing earnest seekers only. They must be able and willing to examine this matter objectively! Religious fanatics and irresponsible enthusiasts may hold aloof, for they are detrimental to the Truth. As for the malevolent and prejudiced, they shall find their sentence in the very words.

The Message will strike only those who still carry within them a spark of truth, and the yearning to be true human beings. To all such it will become the shining light and staff. It will lead them unswervingly out of all the chaos of the present-day confusion.

The following Word does not bring a new religion, but is intended as the torch to help all serious listeners or readers find the right path, which leads them to the longed-for height.

Only he who bestirs himself can advance spiritually. The fool who uses extraneous aids for this, in the form of the ready-made opinions of others, only walks his path as if on crutches, while ignoring his own healthy limbs.

But the moment he boldly uses all the abilities which lie dormant within him awaiting his call, to help in his ascent, he is employing the talent entrusted to him in accordance with his Creator's Will, and will easily overcome all obstacles that seek to divert him.

Therefore awake! Genuine faith lies only in conviction, and conviction comes solely through an inflexible weighing and examining! See that you are truly alive in the wonderful Creation of your God!

Abd-ru-shin

WHAT SEEK YE?

WHAT *seek ye?* What is all this tumultuous agitation? It permeates the world like a ferment, and a flood of books overwhelms all peoples. Scholars pore over ancient writings, investigating and pondering until spiritually exhausted. Prophets arise to warn, to predict . . . suddenly from all sides people strive feverishly to spread new light!

Thus it rages now over the troubled soul of mankind, not refreshing and invigorating, but scorching, consuming, absorbing the last vestiges of strength still left to the afflicted one in this gloominess of the present time.

Here and there also a whispering is heard, rumours of a growing expectation of something impending. Every nerve is restless, tense with subconscious longing. There is seething and surging, and over everything lies a kind of ominously brooding stupor. Fraught with disaster. What *must* it bring? Confusion, despondency and ruin, unless a mighty hand tears asunder the dark layer that now envelops the terrestrial globe spiritually. With the slimy tenacity of a dirty morass, absorbing and smothering every ascending free light-thought before it has become strong; with the gruesome silence of a swamp, suppressing, disintegrating, and destroying every good volition even in the bud, before any action can arise from it.

But the seekers' cry for light, imbued with strength to cleave through the mire, is turned aside and dies away beneath an impenetrable canopy, assiduously set up by the very people who think they help. *They offer stones for bread!*

Look at the innumerable books:

They do not animate, they only weary the human spirit! And this is the proof of the barrenness of all they offer; for whatever wearies the spirit is never right.

Spiritual bread immediately refreshes, Truth revitalises and Light animates!

Simple people must surely despair when they see what walls are being built around the beyond by so-called psychic science. Who among the simple is to grasp the learned sentences and strange expressions? Is the beyond, then, intended exclusively for psychic scientists?

They speak of God! But is it necessary to set up a university in order first of all to acquire the abilities to recognise the conception of the Godhead? To what lengths will this mania, which is mostly rooted only in ambition, drive them?

Readers and listeners stagger along like drunkards from one place to another – unsteady, not free in themselves, one-sided, because they have been diverted from the simple path.

Listen, you despondent ones! Lift up your eyes, you who are seriously seeking: *The way to the Highest lies open to every human being! Proficiency in learning is not the gate to it!*

Did Christ Jesus, that great example on the true path to the Light, choose His disciples among the learned Pharisees? Among the Scribes? He took them from the simple, natural people, because they had no need to struggle against this great delusion that the way to the Light is hard to master, and must be difficult.

This thought is man's greatest enemy, it is a lie!

Thus turn away from all scientific knowledge, where it is a question of what is most sacred in man, which must be *fully grasped!* Leave it alone; for science, being a product of the human brain, is piecework and must remain piecework.

Consider, how should scientific knowledge, acquired by laborious study, lead to the Godhead? *What, after all, is knowledge?* Knowledge is what the brain can conceive. Yet how very limited is the perceptive capacity of the brain, which remains firmly bound to space and time. Even eternity and the meaning of infinity cannot be grasped by a human brain. Just that which is inseparably linked with the Godhead.

But the brain stands silent before the incomprehensible power streaming through all that exists, from which it derives its own activity. The power which everyone intuitively perceives as a matter of course every day, every hour, every moment, whose existence science too has always recognised; whereas with the brain, that is with the knowledge and intellect, one seeks in vain to grasp and comprehend it.

So inadequate is the activity of a brain, the basis and instrument of science, and this limitation naturally also affects what it produces, hence all science it-self. Thus science does indeed *subsequently* help to elucidate, classify and ar-range all that it receives ready-made from the creative power which precedes it; but when it seeks to assume leadership or offer criticism, it must inevitably fail so long as it binds itself so firmly to the intellect, that is, to the perceptive capacity of the brain, as it has done hitherto.

For this reason erudition, along with those who adjust themselves to it, al-ways remains clinging to details; whereas each man carries within himself, as a gift, the great inconceivable whole, and is fully capable of attaining to the noblest and highest without laborious study!

Therefore away with this needless torture of spiritual enslavement! Not for nothing does the great Master exhort us: "Become like children!"

He who bears within himself the firm volition for what is good, and strives to give purity to his thoughts, *has already found the way to the Highest!* All else will then be added unto him. This requires neither books, nor spiritual strain; neither asceticism, nor solitude. He will become sound in body and soul, freed from all pressure of morbid pondering; for all exaggeration is harmful. You are meant to be human beings, not hothouse plants which through one-sided cultivation succumb to the first puff of wind!

Awake! Look around you! Listen to your inner voice! That alone can open the way!

Heed not the dissensions of the churches. The great Bringer of Truth, Christ Jesus, the personification of Divine Love, did not concern Himself with creeds. After all, what are the creeds today? A shackling of the free spirit of man, enslavement of the Divine spark dwelling within you; dogmas that seek to compress the work of the Creator, and also His great Love, into forms moulded by the human mind. This indicates a dishonouring of Divinity, a systematic disparaging.

Every serious seeker is repulsed by such things, because they prevent him from ever experiencing the great reality within himself. As a result his longing for the Truth becomes increasingly hopeless, and finally he despairs of him-self and of the world!

Therefore awake! Shatter the walls of dogma within you, tear off the bandage, so that the pure Light of the Highest may reach you undimmed. Then your spirit will soar aloft in exultation, jubilantly sensing all the great Love of the Father, which knows no limitations of earthly intellect. You will at last know that you are a part of this Love; you will grasp It easily and completely, unite with It, and thus gain new strength daily and hourly as a gift, enabling you to ascend out of the chaos as a matter of course!

THE CALL FOR THE HELPER

JUST let us look more closely at all those people who today with special eagerness are seeking a spiritual helper, those who, inwardly uplifted, are awaiting him. In their opinion they themselves are already thoroughly prepared spiritually to recognise him and to hear his word!

On calm observation we notice a great many factions. Christ's Mission, for instance, affected so many people in a strange way. They formed a false picture of it. As usual, this was due to their wrong self-assessment, their presumption.

Instead of the former veneration and the preservation of a natural gulf and sharp demarcation towards their God, there has arisen on the one hand a plaintive begging which always wants only to receive, but on no account to contribute anything itself. They certainly accepted the "pray", but refused to acknowledge that this was also coupled with "and work" – "work on yourself".

Again, on the other hand, people imagine they are so self-reliant, so independent, that they can do everything themselves, and with a little effort even become Divine.

There are also many people who only demand and expect God to run after them. Inasmuch as He had already once sent His Son, He proved thereby how greatly concerned He is that mankind should draw near to Him, indeed that He probably even needs them!

Wherever one turns there is nothing but presumption to be found in all things, no humility. True self-assessment is lacking. –

In order *really* to be a *human being,* and begin his ascent as *such*, it is first of all necessary for man to descend from his artificial height.

Today, spiritually puffed up, he is sitting in a tree at the foot of the mountain, instead of standing with both feet firmly and securely on the ground. Thus unless he first comes down or falls from the tree he will obviously never be able to climb the mountain.

Meanwhile, however, all those who went their way calmly and sensibly on the ground beneath his tree, and upon whom he looked down so haughtily, have probably arrived at the summit.

But events will come to his aid; for in the very near future the tree *will* fall. When he is so roughly shaken down from his precarious perch, perhaps man will then once more come to his senses. But for him it will then be high time, he has not a single hour left to waste.

Many now think that life can continue in the old way, as it has done for thousands of years. Stretched out comfortably in their armchairs, they are awaiting a strong helper.

But *how* do they depict this helper! It is really pathetic!

In the first place they expect or, just to be quite correct, *demand* that *he* should prepare the way upward to the Light for each individual! *He* must exert himself to build bridges to the path of the Truth for the adherents of *every* religious faith! *He* must make it so easy and intelligible that everyone can understand it without effort. His words must be so chosen that their rightness will immediately convince one and all.

As soon as man must exert himself and think for himself, then the helper is not a proper helper. For if he is called to lead and to show the right way through his word, he must then naturally also exert himself for men. It is *his* duty to convince men, to awaken them! After all, Christ also gave His life.

Those who think in this way today – and there are many who do so – need not begin to trouble themselves, for they are like the foolish virgins, they face the "too late"!

The helper will surely *not* awaken them, but will let them sleep quietly on until the gate is closed and they can find no entrance into the Light, because they cannot free themselves in time from the sphere of matter, for which the word of the helper showed them the way.

For man is not as valuable as he imagined. God does not need him, but he does need his God!

Since in their so-called progress mankind today no longer know what they really *want,* they will at last have to experience what they *must!*

As they both seek and criticise in a supercilious way, this type of people will pass by, just as even at that time so many also passed by *Him* for Whose coming everything had already been prepared through the revelations.

How can one possibly envisage a spiritual helper *thus!*

He will not *budge an inch* to make concessions to mankind, and wherever he is expected to give he will *demand!*

That man who is capable of serious reflection, however, will immediately recognise that *just this strict and uncompromising demand* for attentive thinking contains what is best, and what mankind, already so deeply entangled in spiritual indolence, need for their salvation! It is just by demanding spiritual alertness right from the beginning, together with an *earnest* volition and self-exertion for the understanding of his words, that a helper easily separates the grain from the chaff already at the outset. An automatic working lies in this, as it is in the Divine Laws. Here, too, men receive exactly according to their actual volition. –

But there is yet another class of people who fancy themselves particularly alert!

Naturally these have formed an entirely different picture of a helper, as can be read from reports. It is no less grotesque, however, for they expect him to be ... a spiritual acrobat!

In any case, thousands already suppose that clairvoyance, clairaudience, clairsentience, etc., indicate great progress, which is really *not* so. These arts, whether acquired, cultivated, or even a natural gift, can never rise above the constraint of this earth, thus they only operate within low limits, can never claim to any height, and are therefore almost worthless.

Is *that* the way to help the ascent of mankind – showing them, or teaching them to see and hear, ethereal things which are on the same level as they are?

This has nothing to do with the actual ascent of the spirit, and is to equally little purpose for earthly happenings! They are minor spiritual tricks, nothing more, interesting to the individual, *but utterly useless* to mankind as a whole!

That all such people wish for the same kind of helper, but one even more proficient than themselves, is indeed readily understandable. –

Yet there are a great many who carry matters much further in this respect, even to the point of absurdity. And who are nevertheless perfectly serious about it.

For example, one of the fundamental conditions they impose to prove he is genuine is that a helper ... must be immune from catching a cold! He who does so is already disqualified; for in their opinion this does not correspond to an ideal helper. At all events, a strong helper must as a first essential be completely above these trifles with his spirit.

This may sound fanciful and ridiculous; but it is only based on facts, and suggests a faint repetition of the former cry: "If Thou be the Son of God, save Thyself and come down from the cross!" – They are already calling out the same today, even before such a helper is in sight at all!

Poor, ignorant men! He who trains his body so *one-sidedly* that it is rendered temporarily insensible under the power of the spirit is by no means great or eminent. Those who admire him are like children of former times, watching with open mouth and shining eyes the antics of travelling clowns, and filled with a burning desire to emulate them.

And a great many so-called spirit-seekers or God-seekers of today are no further advanced in the *spiritual* field than the children of bygone days were in this quite *earthly* field!

Just let us consider a little further: The vagrants of olden times, of whom I have just spoken, developed themselves increasingly and became acrobats in circus and music-hall. Their skill grew prodigious, and even now thousands of sophisticated people watch these feats every day in perpetual wonder, often inwardly shuddering.

Yet do they *themselves gain* anything from it? What do they take away with them after such hours? Although many an acrobat even risks his life during his performances. Nothing whatever! For even at the peak of perfection all these things will *always* remain strictly limited to music-hall and the circus. They will always serve only to amuse, but never lead to any advantage for mankind.

Yet people now look for *such* acrobatic feats in the *spiritual* field as the standard by which to measure the great helper!

Let such people keep their spiritual clowns! They will soon enough experience where this leads! They have really no idea *what* they are actually pursuing thereby. They imagine that only he is great whose spirit so controls his body that it no longer suffers illness!

All such development is one-sided, and one-sidedness brings only what is unhealthy and diseased! These things do not *strengthen the spirit,* but only *weaken the body!* The balance necessary for healthy harmony between body and spirit is disturbed, and as a result such a spirit finally severs itself much sooner from the maltreated body, which can no longer provide the strong healthy resonance needed for earthly experience. But then the spirit lacks this experience, and enters the beyond while still *immature*. It will have to live its earth-life *once again*.

These are spiritual tricks, nothing more, performed at the expense of the earthly body, which should in reality *help* the spirit. The body *belongs* to an epoch in the spirit's development. But if it is weakened and suppressed it cannot be of much use to the spirit either; for its radiations are too feeble to provide the full power that the spirit needs in the World of Matter.

If a man wishes to suppress an illness he must spiritually bring about the pressure of an ecstasy on the body, just as in a minor degree fear of the dentist may suppress toothache.

The body may be able to stand such intense stimulation once, perhaps even several times, unharmed, but not continually without suffering serious damage.

And if *that* is the practice or advice of a helper, he is not worthy to be a helper; for he is thereby transgressing the Natural Laws in Creation. Man on earth should cherish his body as property entrusted to him, and strive to achieve healthy harmony between spirit and body. To disturb this through one-sided suppression is neither progress nor ascent, but a decisive obstacle to the fulfilment of his task on earth, as *in the World of Matter* in general. The full power of the spirit as regards its effectiveness *in the World of Matter* is thereby lost, since this definitely calls for the strength of a physical body which is not enslaved but which harmonises with the spirit!

He who is accounted master on such grounds is less than a pupil who knows nothing whatever of the tasks of the human spirit, nor of what is required for its development! He is even detrimental to the spirit.

They will come soon enough to the painful recognition of their folly.

Every false helper, however, will have to undergo *bitter* experiences! His ascent in the beyond can only begin *when the very last* of all those whom he has held up or even led astray by spiritual trifling has come to recognition. As long as his books and writings continue to influence men on earth, he will be held fast in the next world, even if in the meantime he has come to a better understanding there.

He who recommends occult training gives men stones instead of bread, thereby proving that he has not even the faintest idea of what *actually* takes place in the beyond, still less of the complete mechanism of the Universe! –

MEN! WHEN the hour comes in which, according to the Divine Will, the purification and winnowing must take place on earth, then watch for the predicted and partly supernatural signs *in the sky!*

Do not then allow yourselves to be confused by *those* men and also churches who have already long ago surrendered to Antichrist. It is sad that until now not even the churches have known *where* to look for this Antichrist, although he has already been active among all men for so long. If they had only been a little on the alert they must have recognised it! Who can possibly act in a more anti-Christian manner than those who at that time fought against *Christ Himself* and finally also murdered Him! Who could have revealed themselves in a worse and also more obvious way as antagonistic to Christ!

They were the leaders and representatives of earthly religion; and the *true* teaching of God, as revealed in and through the Son of God, did not agree with what they had built up. Indeed, the true Message of God could not be reconciled with it, because the structure set up by priestly dignitaries was aimed at earthly influence, earthly power and expansion.

They proved quite clearly thereby that they were servants of the human intellect, which is directed solely towards earthly knowledge and earthly power, and is hostile and obstructive to everything that lies beyond earthly comprehension! Now since God remains completely outside the range of earthly intellectual knowledge, as also does the spiritual, the intellect is clearly the only real obstacle thereto! Thus by its nature it is opposed to all that is Divine and all that is spiritual! And with it logically therefore all men who acknowledge their intellect as of paramount importance, and seek to build only upon *that!*

The religious leaders of those days were afraid of losing influence among the people through the enlightenment of the Son of God. As everyone today knows, *this* was the main reason for the slanders they sought to spread against

18

Christ, and ultimately also for the execution of the Son of God. They nailed Him to the cross as a blasphemer of the very God by Whom He was sent to bring enlightenment, and Whose servants they professed to be!

They tried to make people believe they were serving God; but how little did they really know *this* God and His Will, for Whose honour and earthly defence this Son of God, the Divine Messenger, was however ... murdered by them!

This was clearly the disastrous result of their enslavement to the earthly intellect, which fought solely to maintain its influence thereby. They allowed themselves to become the executioner as tools of the Antichrist, whom they had secretly enthroned in their hearts. For this satisfied their human weaknesses – their presumption, arrogance and vanity.

Whoever expects clearer proof cannot be helped; for there is nothing more antagonistic to Christ, the Son of God, and His Words! And indeed Antichrist signifies the fighter *against* Christ, against man's redemption in God's Message. The earthly intellect drove them to it! This very intellect, as a poisonous product of *Lucifer,* is an instrument for him which has become the greatest danger to mankind!

Thus the disproportionate over-development of the human intellect in the past has grown into the hereditary sin for man! Behind this, however, stands Lucifer himself as Antichrist in person! *He* it is who through men was able to raise his head! He, the only real enemy of God! He acquired the name of Antichrist through his hostile struggle against the Mission of the Son of God. None other would have had the strength and the power to become the Antichrist.

And in his warfare against the Will of God, Lucifer makes use not merely of *one* man on earth but of nearly all mankind, thus leading them to destruction under the effect of the Divine Wrath! Whoever cannot grasp *this* most obvious fact, that only *Lucifer himself* could be *the Antichrist* who dares to oppose God, will never be able to understand anything of all that takes place outside the World of Gross Matter, that is, outside what is purely earthly.

And as it was then, *so is it still today!* Indeed far worse. Today, too, many religious representatives will wish to fight bitterly to maintain the earthly intellectual ordinances hitherto upheld in the temples and churches.

It is precisely this human intellect, blunting all nobler intuition, that is one of the most insidious growths of Lucifer which he was able to spread among mankind. All slaves of the intellect, however, are in truth *Lucifer's servants*, who are accomplices in the terrible collapse which must thus befall mankind!

Since no one suspected that Antichrist lurked beneath the intellect, he could extend his sinister influence all the more easily! Lucifer triumphed; for he thereby cut off mankind from any comprehending of all that lies outside the World of Gross Matter. From *real life!* From that place where contact is first made with the spiritual, which leads to the proximity of God!

With this he set his foot upon this earth as lord of the earth and of the greater part of mankind!

No wonder, then, that he could penetrate to the altars, and that representatives of earthly religions, also of the Christian churches, were bound to become his victims. For they too expect the Antichrist just before the predicted Judgment. Up till now the great Revelation in the Bible, like many other things, has never yet been understood in this respect.

The Revelation says that this Antichrist *will raise his head* before the Judgment, but not that he will first appear then! If it is said therein that he raises his head, this clearly indicates that he must be here already, but not that he is yet to come. It means that *he will have reached the zenith of his dominion* just before the Judgment!

Listen to this cry of warning, you who are not yet spiritually deaf and blind! Take the trouble for once to think quite seriously about it *yourselves*. If you remain indolent in this respect you give yourselves up as lost!

If you lift the protecting cover from the lair of a poisonous snake that suddenly realises it is exposed, it will naturally try to rear up and bite this ruthless hand.

It is no different here. Finding himself exposed, the Antichrist will quickly protest through his servants; on being unmasked he will make a great outcry, and try in every possible way to maintain himself on the throne which mankind so willingly offered him. But all this he can only do through those who inwardly revere him.

Therefore now keep a sharp watch on your surroundings when the conflict begins! By their very outcry you will all the more surely recognise them, everyone who belongs to him! For once *again,* as before, fear of a pure truth will make them side with its opponents!

The Antichrist will again try desperately to retain his influence on earth. Observe his dubious methods in defence and attack; for he will once more make use only of slander and insinuations, since his followers are incapable of doing anything else. To stand before the Truth and refute it is impossible.

Thus Lucifer's servants will also fight the Messenger of God, just as they once fought the Son of God!

Be on the alert where such an attempt is made; for thereby such people only wish to protect Lucifer in order to uphold his reign on earth. A centre of Darkness lurks there, even if the people habitually appear in bright earthly garments, even if they are servants of a church.

Do not forget what happened when the Son of God was on earth, but reflect that still today the *same* Antichrist, with a far greater human following, is striving to retain dominion over the earth, to escape destruction and to go on obscuring the true Will of God.

Therefore watch carefully for all the promised signs! Each individual must make his *final* decision. Salvation or destruction! For this time it is God's Will that everything which again dares to oppose Him shall be lost!

Every act of negligence will rise up against you in the Judgment! – The Divine Insignia will not appear above some church, nor will any priestly dignitary on earth bear the sign that he is the Messenger of God! But only He Who is inseparably linked with the Signs, Who therefore also carries them living and radiating with Him, as once the Son of God did when He dwelt on this earth. They are the Cross of Truth, living and radiating within Him, and the Dove above Him! They will become visible to all those who are blessed to see spiritual things, so that they may give testimony of it to all people on earth; for there will be among all peoples those who will this time be permitted to "see", as the last Grace of God! – – –

These Sublime Signs of the Holy Truth can never be simulated. Not even Lucifer, who must retreat before them, can achieve this, much less a human being. Therefore he who still seeks to set himself against these Signs of God henceforth sets himself against God as an enemy of God. He shows thereby that he neither is nor ever was a servant of God, no matter what he has hitherto pretended to be on earth.

Be on your guard, lest you also be found among such!

21

MORALITY

It is as though a dark thunder cloud were hanging over humanity. The atmosphere is sultry. Man's intuitive faculty labours sluggishly under a heavy pressure. Only the nerves affecting the senses and animal instincts of the bodies are in a highly-strung condition. Artificially stimulated through the error of a wrong education, of a false attitude, and self-delusion.

In this respect the man of today is not normal, but is burdened with a morbid sexual instinct, aggravated tenfold, for which in a hundred forms and ways he seeks to establish a cult that is bound to become the ruin of all humanity.

Infectious and contagious as a plague, all this gradually influences also those who still seek desperately to cling to an ideal that floats half-hidden in their subconscious mind. They indeed stretch forth their arms longingly towards it, but ever again, after a glance at their surroundings, drop them with a sigh of hopelessness and despair.

Utterly helpless, they observe with horror how swiftly the clear vision regarding morality and bad habits is obscured, how the capacity to judge is lost, and how these concepts change to such an extent that so much which only a short time before would still have aroused disgust and contempt is very soon regarded as quite natural, not even causing surprise.

But the cup will soon be filled to the brim. A terrible awakening must come!

Already now these sensually overwrought masses will sometimes quite involuntarily and unconsciously recoil in sudden misgiving. A momentary feeling of uncertainty grips many a heart; but it brings no awakening, nor any clear perception of their unworthy conduct. They thereupon only redouble their efforts to shake off such "weakness" or "last remnants" of old-fashioned ideas, if not to suppress them altogether.

Progress at any price, that is what it must be. However, one can progress in two directions. Upwards or downwards. As one chooses. And as things now

22

stand it is downwards, with horrifying speed. When the hour strikes for those hurtling downwards to encounter a strong resistance, the impact must shatter them.

In this sultry atmosphere the thunder-cloud grows ever more dense and ominous. At any moment now the first flash of lightning may be expected, rending and lighting up the darkness, and brilliantly illuminating the most obscure corner so relentlessly and sharply as to bring liberation to those striving for light and clarity, but destruction to those who have no longing for the Light.

The longer this cloud has time to grow in darkness and density, the more dazzling and terrifying will also be the lightning it generates. Gone will be the soft enervating atmosphere whose sluggish embrace hides a lurking sensuality; for the first flash of lightning will quite naturally also be followed by a current of fresh, bracing air, bringing new life. In the cold clarity of the light, all the products of morbid imagination will suddenly stand stripped of their dazzling falsehoods before the eyes of horrified humanity.

The awakening will strike the souls like the shock of a mighty thunder-clap, so that the living spring water of undimmed Truth can pour forth and rush over the loosened soil. The day of freedom dawns. Deliverance from the spell of an immorality that has existed for thousands of years, and that is now reaching its climax.

Look around you! Observe what people read, how they dance, how they dress! By tearing down all barriers between the two sexes, the present time is more than ever anxious systematically to obscure the purity of the intuitive perception, thus to distort it and give it misleading masks, and ultimately, if at all possible, to smother it.

When misgivings arise they are quietened by high-sounding talk, which however proves on investigation to emanate only from the inwardly vibrating sexual instinct, in order to provide ever fresh nourishment for the carnal lusts in countless ways, skilful and clumsy, open and covert.

They speak of the emergence of a free independent humanity, of a development of inner stability, of physical culture, the beauty of the nude, ennobled sports, and of education to bring to life the saying: "To the pure all things are pure!" In short: Upliftment of the human race by laying aside all "prudery", thus producing the noble and free human being who is to carry the future! Woe to him who dares to remonstrate! With a great outcry, accusations are immediately hurled at such an audacious person, similar to the assertions that only impure thoughts can make him "find anything wrong in it"!

It is a mad whirlpool of foul water, spreading a stupefying, poisoning atmosphere which, like the effect of morphine, induces mental delusions into which thousands upon thousands continually allow themselves to slide until they become so weakened that they go under.

A brother seeks to enlighten his sister, and children their parents. Like a storm-driven tide it sweeps over all mankind, and wild breakers surge round the few who, gripped with repugnance, have retained their balance and still stand like solitary rocks in the sea. To these cling many whose strength threatens to fail them in the violent storm. It is good to see these small groups standing like refreshing oases in the desert, inviting the traveller to find rest and recuperation after grimly battling his way through the sandstorm that threatened to overwhelm him.

What is being preached today under the fine guise of progress is nothing but a veiled encouragement of utter shamelessness, the poisoning of every higher intuitive perception in man. It is the greatest pestilence that ever befell humanity. And strange: it seems as if so many had only been waiting for a plausible excuse to debase themselves. To countless people it is very welcome!

But he who knows the spiritual laws operating in the Universe will turn away in disgust from today's pursuits. Let us take just one of the "most harmless" pleasures: "Mixed bathing".

"To the pure all things are pure!" These words have such a pleasant sound that many things are permissible under their protection. But just let us consider the most simple ethereal happenings in such a bathing-place. Let us assume that of thirty persons of both sexes, twenty-nine are really pure in every respect. This is an assumption which is completely impossible from the very start; for the opposite would be more correct, and even then still rare. But let us assume it.

Stimulated by what he sees, impure thoughts arise in the mind of the one, the thirtieth bather, although his outward behaviour may be absolutely irreproachable. These thoughts are immediately embodied ethereally in living thought-forms, which move towards and attach themselves to the object of his glances. This is a defilement, whether or not it leads to any remarks or improprieties!

24

The person thus contaminated will carry about this dirt, which is capable of attracting similar straying thought-forms. Thereby they become denser, ever denser around this person, and may finally confuse and poison the victim, as a parasitic creeper often destroys the healthiest tree.

Such are the ethereal happenings in so-called "harmless" mixed bathing, at party games, dances or the like.

It should be borne in mind, however, that in any case it is just all those particularly desirous of having their thoughts and senses excited by such exhibitions who will visit these bathing-places and pleasure haunts! It is not difficult to explain what filth is thus generated, without anyone being outwardly aware of it in the gross material sense.

It is also obvious that this steadily increasing and condensing mass of sensual thought-forms must gradually influence countless people who of themselves do not seek such things. At first vague thoughts of a similar nature arise in them; in time these grow stronger and more alive, being ceaselessly nourished by the various expressions of so-called "progress" around them. And so one after another they glide along into the viscous dark stream, in which the power to apprehend true purity and morality is ever more obscured, until finally everything is dragged into the depth of uttermost darkness.

First of all, these opportunities and incitements for such rapidly growing abnormalities must be done away with! They are nothing but breeding centres into which the pestilential vermin of immoral human beings can cast their thoughts, which then spring up luxuriantly and spread destruction over all humanity; creating ever new breeding grounds which finally form only one huge field of noxious growths, exuding a poisonous stench that also suffocates the good.

Wrench yourselves out of this delirium, which like a narcotic only appears to invigorate, but in reality has a weakening and destroying effect!

It is natural, though sad, that it is just the female sex which is again the first to exceed all bounds, and which has sunk without any scruple to utter shamelessness in their attire.

However, this only proves that the explanation about ethereal happenings is correct. It is just woman, gifted by nature with a stronger intuitive ability, who first and more deeply absorbs this poison of the tainted ethereal world of thought-forms, albeit quite unconsciously. She is more at the mercy of these dangers, for which reason she is also the first to be carried away, and oversteps every limit incredibly quickly and conspicuously.

Not for nothing is it said: "When a woman becomes bad she is worse than a man!" This holds good in everything, be it in cruelty, in hatred or in love! The behaviour of woman will always be a product of the Ethereal World around her! There are exceptions, of course. Nor is woman on this account free from responsibility; for she is able to observe the influences assailing her, and can guide her own volition and actions according to her will if ... she so desires! That the majority of women unfortunately fail to do this is a fault of the female sex, which is entirely due to the absolute ignorance in these matters.

It is a great misfortune for the present time, however, that the future of the people actually lies in the hands of woman. She carries it because her psychic condition influences her descendants more incisively than that of the man. What a decline, then, must the future bring! Inevitably! It cannot be halted by arms, money, nor discoveries. Nor by kindness or diplomacy either. More incisive means are required here.

Yet this enormous guilt does not fall upon woman alone. She will always be only the true reflection of that world of thought-forms which hovers over her people. This must not be forgotten. *Respect and honour* woman *as such*, and she will form herself accordingly; she will become *what you see in her*, and in this way you uplift your whole people!

However, before this can happen, a great process of transformation must take place among women. As they are now a cure can only be effected through a radical operation, by a forceful and relentless intervention, removing any growth with sharp knives and casting it into the fire! Otherwise it would also destroy all the healthy parts.

Towards this essential operation on all mankind the present time is irresistibly rushing, faster, ever faster, and will finally bring it about of itself! This will be painful and terrible, but the end will be restoration to health. Not until then will it be the time to speak of morality. Today it would die away like the word spoken in the wind.

But when the hour is past, in which corrupt Babylon had to perish, because it collapsed from inner decay, then observe the female sex! What they do and what they leave undone will always show you *how you stand*, because through their finer intuitive ability they live what the thought-forms desire.

This fact also gives us the assurance that when the thinking and intuitive perceiving are pure, womanhood will be the first to soar upwards to that ideal which we regard as a truly noble human being. Then morality, in the full glory of its purity, will have entered!

AWAKE!

AWAKE, ye men, out of your leaden slumber! Recognise the ignoble burden you bear, that weighs upon millions with enormous pressure. Throw it off! Is it worth bearing? Not for a single second!

Of what does it consist? Empty husks which the breath of Truth will scatter in the wind. You have wasted time and energy for nothing. Therefore burst the fetters that hold you down, and free yourselves at last!

The man who remains inwardly bound will always be a slave, even if he were a king.

You bind yourselves with all that you aspire to learn. Reflect: In acquiring knowledge you force yourselves into alien forms thought out by others; you willingly adopt an alien conviction, making your own only what others have experienced within, *for themselves.*

Consider: What applies to one does not apply to all! What helps one person may harm the other. Each individual must make his own way to perfection. The abilities he carries within him are his equipment for this. He must adjust himself to them and build upon them! Otherwise he will remain a stranger to his real self, will always stand *beside* what he has learned, which can never come to life in him. Thus he is barred from any gain. He will vegetate, all progress being impossible.

Listen, you who seriously aspire to Light and to Truth:

Each individual must inwardly experience the way to the Light, he must discover it *himself* if he wishes to be sure of the way. Only what a man experiences inwardly, what he perceives intuitively in all its variations, has he fully grasped!

Both sorrow and joy are constantly rapping at the door to encourage and arouse man to awaken spiritually. He is then very often freed for a few seconds from the trivialities of everyday life, and in happiness or grief vaguely senses his affinity with the spirit pulsating through all that lives.

And *everything* is life, nothing is dead! Happy is he who seizes and holds on to such moments of affinity, using them to soar upwards. In so doing he must not keep to rigid forms, but everyone must develop himself, from within.

Ignore the scoffers, who are still strangers to spiritual life. They stand before the great Work of Creation, which offers us so much, like drunkards, like sick people. Like blind men who grope their way through life on earth without seeing all the splendour around them!

They are confused, they sleep; for how can anyone still affirm, for instance, that only what he can see exists? That where his eyes perceive nothing there is no life? That with his physical death he himself also ceases to exist, all because in his blindness he could not, up till now, convince himself to the contrary through his eyes? Does he not already know from many things how very limited is the capacity of the eye? Does he not yet know that it is related to the capacity of his brain, which is bound to time and space? That because of this he *cannot* recognise with his eyes anything rising *above* time and space? Has this logical, intellectual reasoning not yet become clear to any of these scoffers? Spiritual life, let us also call it the beyond, is after all merely something that stands completely above the earthly division of time and space, and therefore requires a similar nature in order to be recognised.

Yet our eyes do not even see all that can be classified within time and space. Think of a drop of water, which appears immaculately pure to every eye; and which on examination under the microscope is shown to contain millions of living organisms mercilessly fighting and destroying each other. Are there not sometimes bacteria in both water and air that have the power to destroy human bodies, and that are imperceptible to the human eye? But they become visible by means of powerful instruments.

Who then will still dare to maintain that there is nothing new and as yet unknown to be seen when the power of these instruments is further increased? Increase their power a thousandfold, a millionfold, and there will be no end to what may be seen, but ever new worlds which previously you could neither see nor feel, yet which nevertheless existed, will unfold before you.

Logical thinking also leads to the same conclusions about everything the sciences have hitherto been able to collect. There is a prospect of continuous progress and development, but never of an end.

What, then, is the beyond? The *word* confuses many. The beyond is simply all that cannot be perceived by earthly means. And earthly means are the eyes, the brain and all other parts of the body, also the instruments that help them to do their work still more accurately and precisely, and to extend its scope.

Therefore one could say: the beyond embraces all that is beyond the perceptive capacity of our physical eyes. *But there is no division between this world and the beyond!* Nor any gulf! All is united, as is the whole of Creation. *One* power streams through this world and the beyond, everything lives and works from this one life stream, and is thus quite inseparably linked. Thus the following becomes clear:

If one part of it sickens the effect must be felt in the other part, as with a physical body. Through the attraction of homogeneous species, diseased matter from this other part will then flow across to the sick part, thus further aggravating the illness. But should such a disorder become incurable, it will absolutely be necessary forcibly to sever the ailing member, if the whole is not to suffer permanently.

For this reason change your attitude. There is no such thing as this world and the beyond, but only one united existence! The idea of a division has been invented solely by man, because he is unable to see everything, and imagines himself to be the centre and focal point of the surroundings visible to him. Yet his sphere of action is greater. With the erroneous idea of a division, however, he forcibly limits himself, hinders his progress, and allows his imagination to run riot and conjure up grotesque pictures.

Is it surprising then, if as a consequence many only smile incredulously, while others adopt an unwholesome form of worship that becomes servile or degenerates into fanaticism? Who can then still be astonished if some people develop a nervous fear, even terror and consternation?

Away with all this! Why these torments? Break down this barrier which human error sought to erect, but which never existed! Your past wrong attitude also gives you a false foundation, on which you vainly endeavour continually to build up the true belief, that is, inner conviction. You consequently encounter points, obstacles, which must make you waver and doubt, or compel you to tear down the whole structure, perhaps abandoning everything out of despair or resentment.

The loss is then yours alone, because this is not progress for you, but standstill or retrogression. The road which in any case you must follow one day will only be lengthened thereby.

When you have at last perceived Creation as a complete whole, as it is, and do not separate this world from the beyond, then you have found the direct path, the true goal draws nearer and the ascent gives you joy and satisfaction. You are then much better able to feel and understand the reciprocal actions pulsating warmly through this uniform whole, since all activity is driven and sustained by the one power. Then the Light of Truth will dawn upon you!

You will soon realise that many who scoff only do so out of indifference and indolence, just because it would require a certain effort to throw over existing ideas and learning and erect something new. Others would find it interferes with their customary mode of living and thus becomes uncomfortable for them.

Leave all such alone, do not argue, but offer your knowledge helpfully to those who are not satisfied with fleeting pleasures, to those who seek for something *more* in their earthly lives than merely to fill their stomachs like animals. Do not then bury your talent, impart to them the recognition you are granted; for in giving, your knowledge will in turn be enriched and strengthened.

An Eternal Law operates in the Universe: That only in giving can one receive where lasting values are concerned! Like a sacred legacy of its Creator, this Law deeply permeates the whole of Creation. To give unselfishly, to help where help is needed, and to understand both the suffering and the weaknesses of your fellow-men, means to receive, because it is the simple and true way to the Highest!

And to will this seriously brings you immediate help and strength! By one single, honest and ardent wish to do good, the wall which your thoughts have hitherto erected as a barrier is cleaved as with a flaming sword from the other side that is now still invisible to you; for you are indeed one with the beyond which you so fear, deny or long for, you are closely and inextricably linked with it.

Try it, for your thoughts are the messengers you send forth, which return heavily laden with similar thought-forms, good or evil as the case may be. This actually happens! Remember that your thoughts are realities that shape themselves spiritually, often becoming forms outliving the earth-life of your body, then much will become clear to you.

Thus it is quite rightly said: "For their works will pursue them!" Thought-creations are works which will one day await you! Which form

31

light or dark rings around you, which you must traverse in order to enter the spiritual world. Neither protection nor intervention can help in this, because the decision lies with you. Therefore you yourself must take the first step in everything. This is not difficult; it lies solely in the volition, which expresses itself through thoughts. Thus you carry heaven or hell within you.

You are free to decide, but you are then irrevocably subject to the consequences of your thoughts, of your volition! You yourselves create these consequences, and that is why I exhort you:

Keep the hearth of your thoughts pure, by so doing you will bring peace and be happy!

Do not forget that every thought you produce and send out attracts all similar thoughts on its way, or attaches itself to others, thus continually increasing in strength and finally also reaching a goal, a human brain which is perhaps off its guard just for a moment, thereby offering such floating thought-forms the opportunity to penetrate and operate.

Just consider what responsibility will fall upon you if at some time or other the thought becomes a deed through some person whom it was able to influence! This responsibility already arises through the fact that every single thought keeps a constant link with you just as if by an unbreakable thread, so as to return with the strength gained on its way, either to burden you or to bring you joy, according to the kind you produced.

Thus you stand in the world of thoughts, and according to your way of thinking at the time make room for similar thought-forms. Do not therefore waste the power of thinking, but gather it for defence and for *keen* thinking, which goes forth like spears and affects everything. Thus create out of your thoughts the *Holy Spear* which fights for the good, heals wounds and furthers the whole of Creation!

Adjust your thinking, therefore, towards activity and progress! To do this you must shake many a pillar supporting traditional ideas.

Often it is some concept wrongly understood that hinders man from finding the right way. He must return to the starting-point. One flash of light will destroy the whole structure so painfully erected over decades, and following a shorter or longer period of stunned inertia, he will make a fresh start! He *must* do so, for there is no standing still in the Universe. Let us take, for instance, the concept of time:

Time passes! Times change! We hear this said everywhere, and automatically a picture arises in the spirit: *We see changing times marching past us!*

This picture becomes so engrained that for many it also forms a solid foundation on which they continue to build, adjusting their whole research and speculation to it. Before long, however, they encounter obstacles which contradict each other. However hard they try, not everything will fit in. They lose their way, leaving gaps that can no longer be filled in spite of all their pondering.

Many then believe that in such places *faith* must act as a substitute for the failure of logical reasoning. But this is wrong! Man should not believe in things he cannot grasp! He must try to understand them; for otherwise he opens wide the door to errors, and with errors the Truth is always debased.

To believe without understanding is just indolence, mental laziness! It does not lead the spirit upwards, but presses it down. Look upward, therefore, we are to test and investigate. Not for nothing does the urge to do so lie within us.

Time! Does it really pass? Why does one encounter obstacles when thinking more deeply about this axiom? Simply because the fundamental idea is *wrong; for time stands still!* We, however, hurry towards it! We rush into time, which is eternal, and seek the Truth in it.

Time stands still. It remains the same, today, yesterday and a thousand years hence! Only the forms change. We plunge into time, to cull from her records for the purpose of enriching our knowledge from what has been collected there! For time has lost nothing, it has recorded all things. It has not changed, because it is eternal.

You too, O man, are always just the same, whether you appear young or old! You remain what you are! Have you not already sensed this yourself? Do you not clearly notice a difference between the form and your "ego"? Between the body that is subject to change and yourself, the spirit, which is eternal?

You seek the Truth! What is Truth? What you still feel to be truth today you will recognise even tomorrow as error, in which, however, you will later again discover grains of truth! For the manifestations also change their forms. Thus your seeking continues, yet amid these changes you mature!

Truth, however, remains always the same, it does not change, for it is eternal! And being eternal it can never be clearly and truly grasped by the earthly senses, which are familiar only with the change of forms!

Therefore become spiritual! Free from all earthly thoughts, and then you will *possess* the Truth, will stand in the Truth, and will bathe in it, constantly surrounded by its pure Light, for it will envelop you completely. As soon as you become spiritual, you will swim in it.

Then you need no longer study so painstakingly what science has to offer, nor need you fear errors, but you will already have the answer to every question in the Truth itself. Moreover, you will no longer have any questions, because without thinking you will know all things, will embrace all things, because your spirit will *live* in the pure Light, in the Truth!

Therefore become spiritually free! Burst all the fetters that hold you down! If obstacles present themselves welcome them joyfully; for they show you the way to freedom and strength! Look upon them as gifts from which you will benefit, and you will overcome them with ease.

Either such obstacles are put in your way to teach and develop you, in which case you add to the means of your ascent, or they are the reaction to some debt you have incurred, which you can redeem in this way and thus free yourselves. In either case they help you to advance. Therefore set out to meet them with a bold heart, it is for your own good!

It is foolish to talk of reverses of fortune or of trials. Every conflict and every sorrow means *progress.* Men are thus offered the chance to dispel the shadows of former misdeeds; for not a single farthing can be remitted to the individual, because here also the cycle of the Eternal Laws in the Universe is inflexible. The Creative Father-Will reveals Himself in them, and thereby forgives us and dispels all Darkness.

So clearly and wisely is everything arranged that the minutest swerving from this would have to plunge the world into ruins.

But what of the man who has very much to redeem from former times, must he not then despair, will he not tremble at the thought of the misdeeds he has to atone for?

As soon as he *honestly wills* he can hopefully and gladly begin with it, free from all worry! For a *balance* can be brought about by the counter-current of the power of good volition, which like other thought-forms takes life in the spiritual, forging a strong weapon capable of removing every dark burden, every weight, and leading the "ego" towards the Light!

Power of volition! A mighty force, unsuspected by so many! Attracting similar powers like a never-failing magnet, it grows like an avalanche.

Uniting with similar spiritual forces, it works backwards, again reaching the starting-point, thus the origin, or rather, the producer, uplifting him high to the Light, or pressing him deeper into the mud and filth! Exactly in accordance with what the author himself originally willed.

He who is acquainted with this steady, never-failing reciprocal effect inherent in all Creation, which manifests and unfolds itself with absolute certainty, knows how to make use of it; he must love it and fear it! Gradually the invisible world around him becomes alive to him; for he feels its influence so distinctly that it silences all doubt.

If he only pays a little attention to it he must intuitively sense the strong waves of ceaseless activity that affect him from out of the great Universe. Finally he feels himself the focal point of strong currents, like a lens that absorbs the rays of the sun, concentrating them on one point and producing a combustive power which can burst forth to singe and destroy, but also to heal, animate and bring blessing; and likewise can start a blazing fire!

And you, too, are such lenses, capable through your volition of gathering these invisible power-currents that reach you, and sending them forth as a united force for good or evil, to bring blessing or indeed destruction to mankind. Through this you can and should light a blazing fire in the souls of men, a fire of enthusiasm for the good, for the noble and for perfection!

This only requires a strength of volition, which in a certain sense makes man lord of Creation and master of his own fate. It is man's own volition which brings him destruction or redemption, reward or retribution, with inexorable certainty!

Do not fear then, that this knowledge will alienate you from the Creator, or weaken your present faith. On the contrary! The knowledge of these Eternal Laws, which you can put to use, makes the entire work of Creation appear even more sublime to you. Its magnitude forces him who searches more deeply to his knees in veneration!

Man will then never wish for evil things. He will joyfully grasp at the best support that exists for him: Love! Love for the whole wonderful Creation, and love for his neighbour, that he too may be led to the glory of this enjoyment, of this consciousness of power.

SILENCE

When a thought suddenly strikes you, keep it back, do not utter it at once, but nourish it; for it will condense through being retained in silence, and gain strength like steam under counter-pressure.

Pressure and condensation produce the quality of a magnetic activity, in accordance with the Law that all that is stronger attracts what is weak. Similar thought-forms are thus attracted from all sides and retained, constantly reinforcing the power of your own, your original thought, yet working in such a way that through the joining of other forms the originally produced form is refined, changes, and takes on different shapes until it comes to maturity. Indeed you sense all this inwardly, but you always think it is entirely your own volition. *But you never give purely your own volition in any matter, there are always other influences as well!*

What does this process tell you?

That only in the union of many elements can anything perfect be created! Created? Is that right? No, but formed! For there is really nothing new to be created; in everything it is merely a matter of producing new forms, since all the elements already exist in the vast Creation. But these elements are to be pressed into service for the way to perfection, which is brought about through union.

Union! Do not pass over this lightly, but try to become absorbed in the concept that maturity and perfection are achieved through union. The principle rests in all Creation as a treasure that needs to be unearthed! It is closely related to the Law that only in giving can there also be receiving! And what is required to grasp these principles aright? Thus to experience them? Love! And therefore love indeed stands as the highest power, as unlimited might, in the mysteries of the great Life!

As with a single thought, union moulds, refines and forms, so is it with man himself and with the whole of Creation, which in a never-ending fusion of existing, individual forms undergoes transformations through the power of volition, and thus becomes the way to perfection.

A single individual cannot offer you perfection, but the whole of humanity, with all its varied characteristics, may do so! Each individual has something which is definitely part of the whole. And this is also why one so far advanced as no longer to know any earthly desires loves all mankind, not one individual, because only the whole of mankind can make the strings of his mature soul, laid bare through purification, sound the chord of heavenly harmony. He bears the harmony within himself, because all strings vibrate!

Let us return to the thought that attracted the other forms, and thereby became strong and ever stronger. It finally emerges beyond you in firmly united power-waves, breaks through your own personal aura, and exerts an influence upon your wider environment.

Mankind call this personal magnetism. The uninitiated say: "You radiate something!" According to your nature, either unpleasant or pleasant. Attractive or repulsive. It is felt!

But you do not radiate anything! The process which engenders the feeling in these others has its origin in the fact that like a magnet you draw to yourself all that is spiritually similar. And it is this drawing that is felt by those around you. Yet in this, too, lies the reciprocal effect. Through the connection the other person then clearly senses your strength, and thereby "sympathy" awakens.

Always bear in mind: Expressed according to our concepts, all that is spiritual is magnetic, and you also know that the stronger always overcomes what is weak through attraction, through absorption. In this way "from him that hath not (the weak one), even that which he hath shall be taken away". He becomes dependent.

There is no injustice in this, but it takes place according to the Divine Laws. Man only needs to pull himself together and will aright, and he will be protected from it.

You will now probably ask: What happens when all want to be strong? When there is nothing left to be taken from anybody? Then, dear friend, *there will be a voluntary interchange,* based on the Law that only in giving can there also be receiving. There will be no standstill on that account, but all that is inferior is eliminated.

Thus it happens that through indolence many become spiritually dependent, and sometimes, in the end, they hardly possess the ability to develop thoughts of their own.

It must be emphasised that only the homogeneous will be attracted. Hence the proverb: "Birds of a feather flock together." Thus drinkers will always find each other, smokers will have "fellow feelings", likewise gossips, gamblers, and so on; yet noble characters will also come together for a high aim.

But it goes further: Whatever is drawn to another spiritually will eventually also manifest *physically,* since everything spiritual penetrates into the gross material, whereby we must bear in mind the Law of Returns, because a thought always remains connected with its origin and radiates back to it through this link.

I am always speaking here only of *real* thoughts, which carry within them the vital power of the psychic intuition. Not of the power wasted by the brain-substance entrusted to you as a tool, which forms but fleeting thoughts that only manifest in a wild medley as shadowy phantoms, and fortunately very soon fade away. Such thoughts merely waste your time and energy, and thereby you fritter away a gift entrusted to you.

If, for instance, you seriously ponder over something, this thought becomes strongly magnetic within you through the power of silence, attracting all that is similar and thus becoming fructified. It matures and rises above the commonplace, thereby even penetrating into other spheres, from which it receives an influx of higher thoughts ... inspiration! Hence, in contrast to mediumship, the basic thought in inspiration must proceed from yourself, must form a bridge to the beyond, to the spiritual world, in order to draw consciously from a spring there. Inspiration has therefore nothing whatever to do with mediumship.

In this way the thought is brought to full maturity within you. You approach its realisation, and *bring* into effect, *condensed through your power,* what already in countless elements was floating in the Universe before as thought-forms.

Through unification and condensation of what has long existed spiritually you thus produce *a new form*! So in the entire Creation it is always only the forms that change, because all else is eternal and indestructible.

Beware of confused thoughts, of all shallowness in thinking. Carelessness will exact a bitter revenge; for it will speedily debase you to the level of a playground for alien influences, through which you very easily become sullen, moody and unjust to your surroundings.

If you have a genuine thought and cling to it, then the gathered power must eventually also press towards realisation; for the evolution of everything takes place entirely in the spiritual, *since every power is purely spiritual!* What then becomes visible to you are always only the final effects of a preceding spiritual-magnetic process, which takes place continually and uniformly according to a firmly established order.

Observation of your thoughts and feelings will soon prove to you that all real life can in truth *only be spiritual life,* in which alone the origin and also the development lie. You must come to the conviction that everything you see with your physical eyes is in reality only the manifestations of the eternally driving spirit.

Every action, even the slightest movement of a human being, is indeed always first spiritually willed. The physical bodies merely act as spiritually animated instruments, which themselves only took shape through the power of the spirit. The same applies to trees, stones and the whole earth. Everything is animated, permeated and driven by the Creative Spirit.

However, since all matter, thus all that can be physically seen, is simply the outcome of spiritual life, it is not hard for you to comprehend that *conditions on earth* are also formed according to the nature of the spiritual life which *immediately* surrounds us. What logically follows from this is clear: Through the wise ordering of Creation man has been given the power to shape conditions for himself with the Power of the Creator. Happy is he who uses it only for good! But woe unto him who succumbs to the temptation to use it for evil!

The spirit in men is only encompassed and darkened by earthly desire, which clings to it like dross, burdens it and drags it down. However, his thoughts are acts of will endowed with spiritual power. *The decision to think in a good or evil way lies with man, and he can thus guide the Divine Power to good or evil purpose!* Therein lies the responsibility that man bears, for reward or retribution will infallibly be his, as all the consequences of his thoughts return to the starting-point through the established reciprocal action, which never fails, and which is quite inflexible in this matter, thus inexorable. Thereby also incorruptible, stern and just! Do people not also say the same of God?

If today many opponents of religion reject the existence of a Godhead, this cannot in any way alter the facts I have cited. People need only omit the little word "God", and engross themselves deeply in science, and they will find *exactly the same*, only expressed in different words. Is it not absurd, therefore, still to argue about it?

There is no getting round the Laws of Nature, no man can defy them. God is the Power that activates the Natural Laws; the Power that nobody has yet grasped or seen, but whose *effects* every one, daily, hourly, indeed in every fraction of a second, must see, intuitively sense and observe, if only he *wants* to do so – in himself, in every animal, every tree, every flower, in every fibre of a leaf swelling and bursting its sheath to come to the light.

Is it not blindness to oppose this so obstinately while everyone, including these stubborn repudiators themselves, confirms and acknowledges the existence of this Power? What is it that prevents them from calling this acknowledged Power God? Is it childlike obstinacy? Or is it a certain shame at being obliged to confess that they have been obstinately trying all the time to deny something, the existence of which has always been clear to them?

Probably nothing of all this. The cause may well lie in the caricatures of the great Godhead held up to mankind from so many sides, which on serious investigation they could not accept. Any attempt to press the all-embracing and all-pervading Power of the Godhead into a picture must certainly debase and dishonour It!

On serious reflection no picture can be brought into harmony with It! Just because every man bears within him the awareness of God, he rejects with misgiving the narrowing down of the great inconceivable Power that created and guides him.

It is *dogma* that is to blame for a great number of those who, in their antagonism, seek to overstep the mark altogether, very often against the certainty living within them.

The hour is not far distant, however, when spiritual awakening will come! When the words of the Redeemer will be rightly interpreted and His great Work of Redemption rightly grasped; for Christ brought redemption from the Darkness by pointing out the way to the Truth, by showing as a man the path to the Luminous Height! And with His blood shed on the cross He set the seal to His conviction!

Truth has never yet been different from what it was even then, and is today, and still will be tens of thousands of years hence; for it is eternal!

Therefore learn to know the Laws contained in the great Book of the entire

Creation. To submit to them means: To love God! For then you will bring no discord into the harmony, but will help to bring the resounding chord to its full magnificence.

Whether you say: I voluntarily submit to the existing Laws of Nature because it is for my own good, or: I submit to God's Will, Which manifests in the Laws of Nature, or to the unfathomable Power Which activates the Laws of Nature ... would the effect be any different? The Power is there and you recognise it, you simply *must* acknowledge it, because as soon as you reflect a little there is nothing else you can do ... and thereby you acknowledge your God, the Creator!

And this Power also operates within you when you are thinking! Therefore do not misuse it to evil purpose, but think good thoughts! Never forget: When you are producing thoughts you are using Divine Power, with which you can achieve the purest and highest!

Try never to forget here that all the consequences of your thoughts always fall back upon you in proportion to the power, importance and extent of the *effect* of the thoughts for good or evil.

Since thought is spiritual, however, the consequences will return *spiritually*. They will thus affect you no matter whether here on earth, or later in the spiritual after your departure. Being spiritual they are by no means bound to the material either. Thus it follows *that the disintegration of the body does not prevent the consequences from taking effect!* The requital in the reaction will surely come, sooner or later, here or hereafter, with all certainty.

The spiritual link with all your works remains firm; for indeed earthly, material works also have a spiritual origin through the creative thought, and will remain in existence even when everything earthly has passed away. It is therefore rightly said: "Your works await you, in so far as the effect has not yet reached you through the reaction".

If you are still here on earth when a reaction is due, or if you are again here, the consequences coming from the spiritual will exert their force *according to their nature* either for good or for evil, through your circumstances and your environment, or directly on yourself, on your body.

Here it must once more be specially emphasised: *The true real life takes place in the spiritual!* And that knows neither time nor space, and therefore no separation either. It stands above earthly conceptions. For this reason the consequences will strike you, wherever you may be, at the time when, according to the Eternal Law, the effect returns to its starting-point. Nothing is lost in the process; it is bound to come.

This now also answers the question so often asked: Why is it that obviously good people must sometimes suffer such bitter adversity in their earth-lives as to make it appear unjust? *These are reciprocal effects, which must strike them!*

Now you know the answer to this question; for your existing physical body plays no part in it. Your body is not you personally, it is not your entire "ego", but an instrument which you have chosen or which you were obliged to take according to the existing Laws of the spiritual life, which you may also call Cosmic Laws if that makes them easier to understand. The particular earth-life is but a short span of your real existence.

A crushing thought if there were no escape, no protecting power to counteract it. On awakening to the spiritual many a person would then have to despair, and wish rather to go on sleeping in the same old way. For he has no idea *what* awaits him, what will still strike him in the shape of reaction from former times! Or as people say: "What he has to make good."

But take comfort! In the wise provision of the great Creation, as you awaken a path is also shown to you through that *power of good volition* to which I have already called special attention, and which mitigates or entirely pushes aside the dangers of the karma that is taking effect.

This, too, the Father's Spirit has given into your hands. The power of good volition forms a circle around you capable of disintegrating the evil pressing upon you, or at least of greatly modifying it, exactly as the atmosphere also protects the earth.

But the power of good volition, this strong protection, is fostered and nourished by the power of silence.

Therefore I once more urgently exhort you, seekers:

"Keep the hearth of your thoughts pure and then, above all, exercise the great power of silence if you wish to ascend."

The Father has already endowed you with the strength for everything! You have only to use it!

ASCENT

You who are striving for recognition, do not entangle yourselves in a web, but become seeing!

Through an Eternal Law you are burdened with an irrevocable obligation to make atonement, which you can never cast upon others. What you burden yourselves with through your thoughts, words or deeds can be redeemed by no one but yourselves! Consider, were it otherwise Divine Justice would be but an empty sound, in which case everything else would also crumble into ruins.

Therefore free yourselves! Do not delay a single hour in setting a limit to this enforced atonement! The honest volition for what is good, for something better, reinforced by a truly heartfelt prayer, *will bring redemption!*

Without the honest, steadfast volition for good there can never be atonement. Evil will then perpetually find ever fresh nourishment to keep it alive, and thus require ever new atonement, unceasingly, so that through constant renewal it only appears to you as a *single* vice or affliction! Whereas it is a whole chain without end, continually binding anew even before the old could be severed.

Then there will never be redemption because of the demand for constant atonement. It is like a chain that keeps you fettered to the ground; and there is very great danger of being dragged still further down. Therefore, you who are still in this world or already in what you regard as the beyond, pull yourselves together at last and concentrate your volition on what is good! With steadfast good volition the end of all atonements *must* come, since he who wills what is good and acts accordingly will incur no fresh debts demanding further atonement. This will then bring deliverance, redemption, which alone permit ascent to the Light. *Listen to the warning! There is no other way for you! For no one!*

But thereby everyone also receives the certainty that it can never be too late. For the individual deed, that you will have to redeem and settle, certainly; yet in the moment when you earnestly begin to strive for the good you mark the end of your atonement. Rest assured that this end *must* come one day, and your ascent will therewith begin! You can then joyfully start working off all your karmaic burden. Whatever you then still encounter is for your own good and brings you nearer to the hour of redemption, of liberation.

Do you now understand the value of my counsel to start exerting yourselves with all your strength for what is good, and to keep your thoughts pure? Not giving up, but pursuing this course with all your longing, all your energy? It will uplift you! It will change you and your environment!

Bear in mind that every life on earth is a short time of schooling, and that you yourselves do not cease to exist when you lay aside your physical body. You will continually live or continually die! Continually enjoy bliss or continually suffer!

Whoever imagines that with earthly burial everything is also ended and balanced for him, may turn and go his own way; for he is only trying to delude himself thereby. Horrified, he will come face to face with the Truth and ... will *have* to begin his path of suffering! His true self, deprived of the protection of his body, whose density surrounded him like a wall, will then be attracted, enveloped and held fast by what is homogeneous.

It will be more difficult for him, and for a long time impossible, to arouse the earnest volition for what is better, which could liberate and help him to ascend, because he is entirely subject to the influence of the homogeneous surroundings, which does not carry the kind of light-thought that might awaken and support him. He must suffer doubly under everything he has created for himself.

For this reason ascent is much harder than when he was in the flesh, where good and evil dwell side by side, which only the protection of the physical body makes possible because ... this earth-life is a school in which every "ego" is given the opportunity of further development according to its free will.

Therefore rouse yourselves at last! The fruit of every thought will return to you, here or there, and you have to taste of it! No one can escape this fact!

Of what use is it to try and bury your head timidly in the sand like an ostrich, to evade this reality? Face the facts boldly! You thereby make it easy for yourselves; for here progress is quicker.

Make a start! But realise that all old debts must be settled. Do not expect blessings to rain down upon you immediately, as many fools do. Perhaps some of you still have a long chain to expiate. But he who despairs on that account only harms himself, because it cannot be spared and remitted him. Through hesitation he only makes everything more difficult for himself, perhaps for a long time impossible.

This should spur him on not to delay another hour; for he only begins to live when he takes the first step! Happy is he who plucks up the courage to do so, for link by link he will be released. He can rush ahead with giant strides, jubilantly and gratefully overcoming also the last obstacles; for he becomes free!

The stones that his previous wrong-doing had heaped up before him like a wall, *inevitably* barring his advance, will indeed not be cleared away, but on the contrary will be carefully laid out before him so that he may recognise and surmount them, because he must bring about the balance for all his errors. However, filled with astonishment and admiration, he will soon see the love that surrounds him as soon as he only evidences his goodwill.

With tender forbearance the way will be made as easy for him as a child's first steps, aided by its mother. Should there be things in his former life that were a silent source of apprehension to him, and which he would rather let sleep forever ... quite unexpectedly he will be placed directly before them! He must decide, must act. In a striking way he is urged to do so through the enchainments. If he then ventures to take the first step, trusting in the victory of the good volition, the fateful knot is severed, he passes through and is freed from it.

But hardly is this debt settled than already the next one in some form or other presents itself to him, requesting as it were also to be settled.

Thus one by one the fetters that restricted and were bound to weigh him down are burst. He feels so light! And the feeling of lightness which some of you have surely experienced at one time or another is no illusion, but the effect of reality. The spirit thus freed from pressure becomes light and, in accordance with the Law of Spiritual Gravity, leaps upwards, to that region to which in accordance with its lightness it now belongs.

And so it must rise steadily upwards towards the longed-for Light. An evil volition presses the spirit down and makes it heavy, whereas a good volition uplifts it.

For this, too, Jesus has already shown you the simple way leading unerringly to the goal; for deep truth lies in the simple words: *"Love thy neighbour as thyself!"*

With these words He gave the key to freedom and ascent! Because it is an irrefutable fact: What you do for your neighbour you do in reality only for yourselves! Solely for yourselves, since according to the Eternal Laws everything returns to you without fail, good or evil, either already here or there. It will surely come! Thus you are shown the simplest of ways in which this step to the good volition is to be understood.

You should give to your neighbour with your *being*, your nature! Not necessarily with money and goods. For then those without means would be excluded from the possibility of giving. And in this being, in this "giving yourself" in the relation with your neighbour, in the consideration and respect you voluntarily offer him, lies the "love" of which Jesus speaks; lies also the help you give to your neighbour, because it enables him to change himself or ascend further, and because he gains strength from it.

The returning radiations of this, however, will quickly uplift you in their reciprocal action. You will receive continually new strength through them. With a soaring flight you will then be able to strive towards the Light ...

Poor fools are they who can still ask: "What do I gain by giving up so many old habits and changing myself?"

Is it a question of a business deal? And were they only to gain as human beings, to become ennobled as such, that alone would be reward enough. But there is infinitely more to it! I repeat: The moment a man begins to exert his good volition he also marks the end of his obligation to make atonement, which he must fulfil and can never escape. In this respect no one else can take his place.

Thus with this resolution the end of the enforced atonement is in sight. Of such great value is this that all the treasures of this world cannot outweigh it. He thus struggles free from the chains that fetter him, which he is constantly forging for himself. Therefore rouse yourselves from your enervating sleep. Let the awakening come at last!

Away with the intoxication that brings the paralysing delusion that redemption through the Saviour has become a letter of safe conduct, enabling you to spend your whole life in careless selfishness, provided that in the end you embrace the faith, turn back, and depart this earth believing in the

Saviour and His Work! Fools to expect such miserable, defective piecework from the Godhead! That indeed would mean cultivating evil! Remember this, and free yourselves!

CULT

CULT should be the endeavour which has taken on form, to make in some way acceptable to the earthly senses something that is beyond earthly comprehension.

It *should* be the endeavour which has taken on form, but unfortunately this is not yet so; for otherwise many things would have to have quite different forms if they had *emerged* from the endeavour itself. The *right* way for this requires the breaking forth of the outward forms from the inmost being. But all we see today is an *intellectual* upbuilding, into which the intuitive perceptions are only *afterwards* to be pressed. Thus the opposite way is taken, which naturally might just as well be called the reverse or wrong way, that can never really be inwardly alive.

As a result many a thing appears clumsy or obtrusive, which in another form would come much nearer to the *real* volition, and only then could have a convincing effect.

Much that is well-intentioned must repel rather than convince, because the right form for it has not yet been found, which the intellect can never give for something that is beyond earthly comprehension!

So is it also in the churches. The intellectual upbuilding here, which is directed towards earthly influence, is only too evident, and much that is good fails to impress because it has an unnatural effect.

On the other hand only that which does not conform to the Laws of Creation can have an unnatural effect. Just such things, however, are very much in evidence in the present-day cults, where simply everything that is opposed to the natural Laws of Creation is shrouded in a mysterious darkness.

However, just by unconsciously never speaking of a mysterious light in such matters, but always only of a mysterious darkness, men strike the right note; for the Light knows no veiling, therefore also no mysticism either, which should have no place in the Creation that arose out of the perfect Will of God, and works automatically in accordance with an unchangeable rhythm. Nothing is more clear in its weaving than just Creation, which is the Work of God!

Therein lies the secret of success and continuity, or of collapse. Where something is built on these living Laws of Creation, there they help, bring success and also continuity. But where these Laws are not observed, either through ignorance or self-will, sooner or later collapse must inevitably follow; for nothing that does not stand on a firm and solid foundation can endure permanently.

That is why so much of man's work is transient when it need not be so. This includes many kinds of cults, which have to undergo continual changes to prevent them from complete collapse.

In the simplest and clearest manner, the Son of God gave to earthmen in His *Word* the *right* path on which to lead their lives on earth in accordance with this weaving of Creation; so that through the Laws of God that operate in the weaving of Creation they might be helped, sustained and uplifted to Luminous Heights, and so also attain to peace and joy on earth.

Unfortunately, however, the churches have not followed the way to the redemption and upliftment of mankind, quite clearly explained and given to them by the Son of God Himself. Instead they have added to His teaching many of their own ideas as well, thereby naturally creating confusion, which was bound to cause dissensions because it was not in accordance with the Laws of Creation, and therefore, strange as it may sound, is also opposed to the clear teaching of the Son of God, although they call themselves Christians after Him.

So is it, for example, with the mariolatry of the papal Christians. Did Jesus, Who taught men *everything,* how they should think and act, yes even speak and pray, in order to do what is right and what lies in the Will of God, ever say even one single word of the kind? *No, He did not!* And this is a proof that He did not wish it either, that it was not to be!

There are even statements by Him which prove the opposite of what mariolatry implies.

And surely Christians would wish through honest living to follow only Christ, otherwise they would not *be* Christians.

If still more has now been added by men, and the papal churches act otherwise than as Christ taught, it is proof that this church has the effrontery to set itself *above* the Son of God; for it tries to improve on His Words by instituting practices which the Son of God did *not* want, because otherwise He would undoubtedly also have taught them, judging by all He gave to men.

Certainly, there *is* a Queen of Heaven, Who according to earthly conceptions could also be called the Primordial Mother, and Who yet possesses the purest virginity. She however has dwelt from all eternity in the *Highest Heights,* and has never been incarnated in an earthly body!

And it is She, Her *radiated picture,* but not in reality Herself, that can occasionally be "seen" or "intuitively perceived" by persons who have been profoundly moved. Through Her, help often comes at such an accelerated speed that people call it a miracle.

However, it is never possible, even for the most matured human spirit, to have an actual vision of this Primordial Queen *Herself,* because in accordance with the inflexible Laws of Creation each species can only always see the same species. Thus the physical eye can only see earthly things, the ethereal eye only ethereal things, the spiritual eye only spiritual things, and so on.

And since the human *spirit* can only see the spiritual, from which it has emerged, it is unable actually to behold the Primordial Queen, Who is of a much higher species. But should anyone ever be so blessed, it would *only* be possible to see *Her spiritually radiated picture.* This, however, appears so lifelike, and can be so strong even in its radiation, that it works miracles wherever it finds the soil prepared for it, through unshakable faith or the deep emotions arising out of suffering or joy.

This lies in the working of Creation, which issues from and is sustained by the perfect Will of God. In this working also lies all help for men from the beginning and unto all eternity, providing they themselves do not turn away from it in their pretentious learnedness.

God manifests in Creation; for it is His perfect Work.

And it is just on account of this perfection that the earthly birth of the Son of God had also to be preceded by a physical procreation. Whoever asserts the contrary throws doubt on the perfection of the *Works* of God, and thus also on the perfection of God Himself, out of Whose Will Creation issued.

An *immaculate* conception is a conception in purest love, as opposed to a conception in sinful lust! But no earthly birth without procreation.

If an earthly conception, that is, a physical procreation as such could not be immaculate, then every motherhood would have to be regarded as unclean!

Through Creation God also speaks, and clearly shows His Will.

To recognise this Will is the duty of man. And the Son of God in His Holy Word showed the right way to do so, because men had made no effort towards it, and had thus entangled themselves more and more in the self-acting Laws of Creation.

This inflexible weaving of Creation was bound to destroy men in time through their ignorance and misapplication; whereas it will raise mankind on high if they live aright according to the Will of God.

Reward and punishment for man lie in the weaving of Creation, which is perpetually and unswervingly guided by the Will of God Itself. In it also lies rejection or redemption! It is relentless and just, always impartial, never arbitrary.

In it lies the indescribable Greatness of God, His Love and Justice. That is, in *His Work,* which He made over to man and to many other beings, as a dwelling-place and a home.

The time has now come for men to acquire the *knowledge* of it, so that with complete conviction they will come to the recognition of *God's activity,* which is expressed in His *Work!*

Then every earthman will stand quite unshakable here on earth, filled with the most joyful eagerness to work, most gratefully looking up to God, because recognition links him for all time through the *knowledge!*

In order to convey to mankind such knowledge, which gives them a clear and intelligible conviction of the working of God in His Justice and Love, I have written the work "In the Light of Truth", which leaves no gap, contains the answer to *every* question, and clearly shows to mankind how wonderful are the ways in Creation that are upheld by many servants of His Will.

But God alone is Holy!

Everything in Creation is movement. Brought into being strictly according to Law by the pressure of the Light, movement produces heat through which forms are able to unite. Thus without Light there could be no movement, and therefore man can also imagine that in the proximity of the Light the movement must even be far more rapid and strong than at a vast distance from It.

In fact the greater the distance from the Light, the slower and more sluggish becomes the movement. In time it may even lead to the rigidity of all the forms which had already taken shape when at first the movement was still more animated.

The expression "Light" in this connection does not, of course, refer to the light of some planet, but to the *Primordial Light,* which is Life itself, therefore God!

Following this picture of a great survey of what takes place in Creation, I wish for once today to direct attention to the earth, which is now revolving at a far greater distance from the Primordial Light than it did many millions of years ago, because it has been increasingly exposed to the weight of the Darkness through men, who in their ridiculous and stubborn conceit, due to a one-sided over-development of the intellect, drew away from God. The intellect is and will always continue to be directed only *downwards* towards coarse matter, because *that is the purpose* for which it was provided; on the assumption, however, that it should be able to receive absolutely undimmed all radiations and impressions emanating from above, out of the Luminous Heights.

All the work of the intellect for outward activity in coarsest matter, that is, in material substance, falls to the frontal brain. On the other hand, the back brain has the task of taking in from above impressions which are lighter and more luminous than coarse matter, and passing them on for further use.

This harmonious co-operation of the two brains, given to men for their benefit, was disturbed by man's one-sided surrender to purely earthly, that is, to gross material activities. In the course of time it was completely stifled and tied off, as it were, because owing to its excessive activity the frontal brain was bound gradually to over-develop in proportion to the neglected back brain, which consequently became still less capable of receiving and also weakened. Thus over thousands of years the *hereditary evil* came into being through physical reproduction; for even newly-born children brought with them a frontal brain proportionately far more developed than the back brain. This held the danger of the awakening of the *hereditary sin,* through which man is compelled from the outset to direct his thoughts solely towards earthly things, and thus away from God.

All this will be easily comprehensible to every man of sincere good-will; moreover, I have given many and detailed explanations of it in my Message.

All the evil on earth came into being because man, owing to his spiritual origin, could exert a pressure with his volition upon everything else existing on earth; whereas just because of this spiritual origin he could and also should have had an *uplifting* influence; for that was and is his real task in Subsequent Creation, in which all that is spiritual naturally takes the lead. It can lead upwards, which would be the natural thing, but it can also lead downwards if the volition of the spiritual is mainly striving only after earthly things, as is the case with earthmen.

In the knowledge of Creation which I have given in my Message, and in the related explanation of all the Laws automatically working in Creation, which may also be called the Laws of Nature, the whole weaving of Creation is displayed without a gap; it allows every process to be clearly recognised, and therewith the purpose of man's whole life. With unassailable logic it also unfolds his "whence" and his "whither", thus giving an answer to every question, provided man seriously seeks for it.

Even the most malevolent opponents must halt here, because their cunning is insufficient to be able to invade and destroy the perfect completeness of what has been said, and thus also rob man of this help. – –

I have said that the movement in Creation must become progressively slower the further away anything is from the Primordial Light, the starting-point of the pressure which subsequently brings about movement.

So is it with the earth at the present time. Through the guilt of earthmen its orbits have become increasingly distant. As a result the movements are be-

53

coming slower, ever more sluggish, and thereby much has already approached the stage where rigidity sets in.

Rigidity also has very many stages; in its beginnings it is not so easy to recognise. Even while it is progressing, recognition remains impossible unless a flash of light for once stimulates the keenest observation.

This recognition is difficult simply because everything living within the sphere of the steadily slackening movements is also drawn uniformly into the increasing denseness that leads to rigidity. This applies not only to the body of a human being, but to everything, including his thinking. It affects even the most minute things. Imperceptibly every concept also changes and becomes distorted, even those concerning the actual meaning of the language.

Since he himself is drawn along in the same sluggish vibration, man cannot notice this in his neighbour, unless from out of his inner being he seeks once more to fight his way upwards spiritually with the strongest volition and with tenacity, so as again to come a little nearer to the Light. His spirit will then gradually become more mobile, thus lighter and more luminous, and will influence his earthly recognition.

Terrified and aghast with horror, however, he will then see, or at least intuitively perceive, how far the distortions of all concepts have already progressed in rigidity on this earth. The far-seeing view of how things really are is lacking, because everything has been pressed into narrow and obscure limits which can no longer be penetrated, and must in time completely stifle everything they embrace.

I have already often pointed out distorted concepts; but now, through the steady withdrawal from the Light, these are slowly proceeding on the downward path to rigidity.

It is unnecessary to give individual examples, for either no attention whatever would be paid to such explanations, or they would be described as tiresome quibbling, because man is much too rigid or too indolent to want to give them serious reflection.

I have also already spoken sufficiently of the power of the word, of the mystery that even the *human word* can, for a time, work constructively or destructively on the weaving of Creation within the sphere of the earth. This is because through the sound, tone and composition of a word, creative forces are set in motion which do not work according to the intention of the speaker, but according to the sense of the *word* in its meaning.

The meaning, however, was originally given through the forces which the word sets in motion, and which are therefore exactly adjusted to the *true* meaning, or vice versa, but not to the volition of the speaker. Meaning and word arose out of the corresponding movement of forces, therefore they are inseparably *one!*

Again, man's *thinking* sets in motion *other* currents of force which correspond to the essence of his thinking. Man should therefore endeavour to choose the right words to express his thinking, thus in so doing to perceive intuitively in a more accurate and clear manner.

Suppose a man is asked about something of which he has heard, and part of which he may even have seen. When questioned he would maintain without hesitation that he *knows* it!

In the opinion of many superficial people this answer would be correct, and yet in truth it is *wrong* and objectionable; for "to know" means to be able to give *exact information* about everything, every detail from beginning to end, without any omission and from one's own experience. Only *then* can a man say that he *knows* it.

Great responsibility attaches to the expression, and to the concept of "knowledge" associated with it!

I have also already pointed out the great difference between "knowledge" and what has been "learned". Learnedness is by no means real *knowledge,* which can only be absolutely personal; whereas what has been learned remains the acceptance of something outside the personal.

To hear something, and perhaps even to see part of it, is far from being the *knowledge* itself! A man should not assert: I *know* it, but the most he could say is: I have heard of it or seen something of it. If he wishes to act *correctly,* however, truth would oblige him to say: I do not know it!

This would be far more correct in every way than to report about something which he himself has nothing to do with, and which cannot therefore be a real *knowledge* either; whereas through incomplete reports he would only cast suspicion on or incriminate other people, perhaps even plunge them unnecessarily into misfortune, without knowing the actual ins and outs. Therefore carefully weigh with your intuitive perception *every* word you intend to use.

He who thinks more deeply, who will not be satisfied with already rigid concepts as a personal excuse for loquacious pomposity and malevolence, will easily understand these explanations, and in quiet examination will learn to look further in everything he says.

A multitude of such restricted concepts, with their fatal consequences, have already become habitual among earthmen. They are greedily snatched up and promoted by slaves of the intellect, who are the most willing adherents of the Luciferian influences of deepest Darkness.

Learn to observe attentively and to use properly the currents in this Creation, which bear the Will of God, and thus God's Justice in pure form. Then you will again find the true humanity which has been wrested from you.

How much suffering would thereby be avoided, and how many ill-disposed persons among mankind would also be deprived of the opportunity to commit their deeds.

This evil is also responsible for the description of the earthlife of the Son of God Jesus not corresponding at all points with the facts, as a result of which a totally false picture has gradually arisen in the minds of men up till now. The words given by Him were also distorted, as has happened with *every* teaching that was made into a religion and which was intended to bring upliftment and perfection of spirit to mankind.

And therein also lies the great confusion among all men, who increasingly fail really to understand one another, thus allowing discord, distrust, slander, envy and hatred to grow and flourish.

All these are unmistakable signs of advancing rigidity on earth!

Arouse your spirit, and begin to think and speak in a *far-seeing* and comprehensive way! This naturally also demands that you not only work with the intellect, which belongs to coarsest matter, but also make it possible once more for your spirit to guide your intellect, which should serve the spirit as ordained by your Creator, Who from the very beginning has permitted you to come undistorted into existence here on earth.

So much is already in the first stage of rigidity. Soon your entire thinking may already be gripped by it and must flow through rigid, iron channels, bringing you nothing but uneasiness, suffering upon suffering, and finally forcibly degrading you from a human being to the state of an empty machine serving only the Darkness, far away from all Light. –

THE WORD "childlike" is an expression which is in most cases wrongly applied by human beings in their careless and thoughtless manner of speaking.

Hampered by indolence of the spirit, this expression is not perceived intuitively enough to be properly grasped. But he who has not grasped it in its entirety will never be able to use it aright either.

And yet it is just childlikeness that offers mankind a strong bridge for ascent to Luminous Heights, for giving every human spirit the possibility to mature, and for reaching perfection in order to live eternally in this Creation, which is the House of God the Father that He places at the disposal of men, provided ... they remain guests therein who are *agreeable* to Him. Guests who do not cause damage in the rooms so graciously made over to them solely for their use, with a table at all times richly spread.

But how far removed is man now from the childlikeness he so needs!

Yet without it he can achieve nothing for his spirit. The spirit *must* possess childlikeness; for it is and remains a child of Creation, even when it has gained full maturity.

A child of Creation! In this lies the deep meaning; for the spirit must develop into a child of God. Whether it will ever achieve this depends entirely on the degree of recognition it is willing to acquire on its wanderings through all the Spheres of Matter.

But with this willingness the *deed* must also manifest. In the Spiritual Planes will is at the same time also deed. There will and deed are always *one*. However, this is only so in the *Spiritual* Planes, not in the Worlds of Matter. The more dense and heavy a plane of the World of Matter is, the further removed is the deed from the will.

The fact that density causes obstruction is demonstrated even by sound, which as it travels has to struggle through material substance, which obstructs it according to the nature of the density. This can be clearly observed even over shorter distances.

When a man chops wood or drives nails into the timbers of a building, the impact of his tool can be clearly seen, yet the sound of it only arrives a few seconds later. This is so noticeable that everybody must have experienced it at one time or another.

The process is similar, but still more ponderous, between the will and the deed of man on earth. The will flares up in the spirit, and is immediately deed in the spirit. But to make the will visible in the Gross Material World, the spirit also needs the physical body. Only on impulse does a physical body already act within a few seconds of the flaring up of the will. Thereby the more tedious work of the frontal brain is eliminated, which otherwise has to mediate the way of the will right up to the impression on the activity of the body.

The normal way takes rather longer. Sometimes the result is only a feeble action, or none at all; because on its extended way the volition is weakened, or altogether suppressed, by the pondering intellect.

In this connection, although not strictly relevant here, I would like to make a reference to the effects of Creation's Law of the Attraction of Homogeneous Species, which are overlooked and yet so clearly visible also in human activity:

Human-earthly laws have been worked out by the earthly intellect, and are also carried into effect by it. *For this reason* schemes pondered with the intellect, thus premeditated actions, are as such more severely punished and judged as more evil than actions committed on the impulse of the moment, thus unpremeditated. In most cases these latter are treated more leniently.

In reality, there is a connection which is imperceptible to men, in the homogeneity of intellectual activity under the compulsion of the Law of Creation, for all those who unconditionally submit to the intellect. To them this is quite understandable.

Without knowing about it, the greater part of the atonement for an impulsive action is therewith assigned to the *Spiritual Plane*. Legislators and judges have no idea of this, because they proceed from quite different, purely intellectual principles. With deeper reflection, however, and knowledge of the active Laws of Creation, all this appears in an entirely different light.

Nevertheless, in other earthly sentences and judgments, the Living Laws of God in Creation work quite independently on their own, uninfluenced by earthly-human laws and conceptions. It will surely not occur to any serious-minded person to think that real guilt, not merely what men first designate as guilt, could also be expiated at the same time before the Laws of God through a paid penalty dictated by the earthly intellect!

Already for thousands of years these have been, as it were, two separate worlds, separated by men's actions and thoughts, although they should only be *one* world in which *God's* Laws alone operate.

Through such earthly punishment, atonement can only ensue if the laws and the punishments are completely in accord with God's Laws in Creation.

Now there are two kinds of unpremeditated actions. Firstly, those already described, which should really be called *impulse;* and then the kind that flashes up in the frontal brain, thus not in the spirit, and belongs to the intellectual category. The latter are unpremeditated, but should not receive the same mitigation as impulse-actions.

However, to find out exactly the just difference between the two will only become possible to *those* human beings who know all the Laws of God in Creation and are familiar with their effects. This must be reserved for a time to come, when there will also be no more arbitrary actions among men, because they will have a spiritual maturity that lets them swing only in the Laws of God in all their deeds and thoughts.

This digression is merely to induce reflection, it did not belong to the real purpose of the lecture.

Take note, then, that in the Spiritual Planes will and deed are *one,* but in the Material Planes they are separated through the nature of the substance. That is why Jesus once said to men: *"The spirit is willing, but the flesh is weak!"* The flesh, which refers here to the gross material substance of the body, does not convert into deed everything that has already been will and deed in the spirit.

But also on earth the spirit in its gross material garment could compel its volition always to become a gross material deed, if it were not too lazy to do so. It cannot hold the body responsible for this indolence; for the body was given to each spirit only as an instrument, which it must learn to control in order to use it properly. –

Thus the spirit is a child of Creation. And it must be *childlike* therein if it wishes to fulfil the purpose for which it stands in Creation. The arrogance of the intellect caused the spirit to withdraw from childlikeness, because the intellect could not "understand" what it really is. As a result, however, the spirit lost its foothold in Creation, which in order to remain healthy itself must now expel it as a stranger, an intruder and a dangerous creature.

And so it will come to pass that through their wrong thoughts and actions men will dig their own graves. –

How strange it is that every man who wishes to experience the Christmas Festival in the true sense must first try to recall his childhood!

This can surely be regarded as a clear enough sign *of the fact* that as an adult he is quite incapable of experiencing the Christmas Festival with his *intuitive perception*. It is definite proof that he has lost something he possessed as a child! Why does this not make men reflect!

Again it is spiritual indolence that prevents them from serious reflection on such matters. "That is for children," they think, "and grown-ups have simply no time for it! They have to think about *more serious matters.*"

More serious matters! By these more serious matters they mean only the pursuit of earthly ends, thus the work of the intellect! The intellect quickly represses memories, so as not to lose its supremacy if the intuitive perception is for once yielded to!

The *greatest* things could be recognised in all these apparently so trivial facts, if only the intellect would allow time for it. But it has the upper hand, and fights for it with all craftiness and cunning. That is to say, it is not the intellect that fights, but actually that which uses it as a tool and hides behind it: the Darkness!

The Darkness does not want the Light to be found in memories. And *how* the spirit longs to find the Light, to draw new strength from It, can be recognised by the fact that with the memories of childhood Christmas Festivals there also awakens an undefined, almost painful longing, able to move many people for a brief moment to tenderness.

If such tenderness were used at once and with all one's strength, it could become the best soil for the *awakening!* But unfortunately this only sends adults into a reverie, whereby the rising power is wasted and lost. And in the reverie the opportunity also slips by without the possibility of bringing benefit, or of having been used.

Even though many a person sheds a few tears, he feels ashamed and tries to hide them, pulling himself together with a physical jerk that so often betrays unconscious defiance.

How much could people learn from all this. It is no coincidence that a tender sadness also weaves itself into the memories of childhood days. It is the subconscious sensing that something has been lost, leaving an emptiness, the inability still to perceive intuitively like a child.

But you have surely often noticed the wonderful and refreshing influence of the mere quiet presence of any person from whose eyes a *childlike* radiance sometimes glows.

The adult must not forget that childlike is not childish. But you do not know whence the childlike has such an effect, what it really is! And why Jesus said: "Become as little children!"

To fathom what childlike is, you must first be clear that the childlike is by no means bound up with the child itself. No doubt you yourselves know children who lack the true beautiful childlikeness! Thus there are children without childlikeness! A malicious child will never have a childlike effect, nor an unruly one who is really ill-bred!

This clearly shows that childlikeness and the child are two things independent in themselves.

That which is called childlike on earth is a branch of the effect from out of *Purity!* Purity in its higher, not merely earthly-human sense. The human being who lives in the ray of Divine Purity, who makes room for the ray of Purity within himself, has thereby also acquired childlikeness, whether it be still in childhood or already as an adult.

Childlikeness is the result of inner purity, or the sign that such a human being has submitted to Purity and serves It. All these are merely different modes of expression, but in reality they always amount to the same thing.

Thus only a child who is pure within itself, and an adult who cultivates purity within himself, can have a childlike effect. That is why he has a *refreshing* and vitalising effect, and also inspires confidence!

And wherever there is true purity, genuine love can also enter, for God's Love works in the ray of Purity. The ray of Purity is the path It treads. It could not possibly walk on any other.

The ray of Divine Love can never find its way to him who has not absorbed the ray of Purity!

Man, however, has deprived himself of childlikeness by turning away from the Light through his one-sided intellectual thinking, to which he has sacrificed everything that might have uplifted him. Thus he has firmly chained himself with a thousand fetters to this earth, that is, to the World of Gross Matter, which will hold him in its grip until he liberates himself from it. This, however, cannot come to him through earthly death, but only through *spiritual* awakening.

CHASTITY

CHASTITY is a concept that has been so unbelievably narrowed down by earthmen that absolutely nothing of its real meaning is left. It has even been dragged on to a wrong course; and as the natural and inevitable consequence this distortion has brought needless oppression, and even very often untold suffering, upon many people.

Ask where you will what chastity is, and everywhere in reply you will find explained in one way or another the concept of physical virginity; in any case, this is the highest that the perception of earthmen can reach.

This proves completely the inferior way of thinking of those who subordinate themselves to the intellect, which has itself set the limits to everything earthly, because it cannot reach any further with its faculties that are born of the earthly.

How easy it would then be for man to be regarded as chaste and so create a reputation, while sunning himself in vain self-glorification. But this does not bring him one step upwards on the road to the Luminous Gardens, which as Paradise are the blissful and final goal of a human spirit.

It is of no avail to earthman if he keeps his physical body chaste and defiles his spirit, which can then never cross the thresholds that lead upwards from one step to the next.

Chastity is different from men's idea of it, far more comprehensive and greater. It does not demand that man should go against nature; for this would be an offence against the Laws vibrating in God's Creation, and could only have harmful results.

Chastity is the *earthly* concept of Purity, which is *Divine*. For every human spirit it is the endeavour to manifest gross-materially what is sensed as a reflection of something that really exists in the Divine Sphere. Purity is Divine, chastity its representation by the human spirit; thus a spiritual image, which can and should become evident in earthly conduct.

This should suffice as a fundamental Law for every *matured* human spirit in order to realise chastity. But on earth, urged on by many a selfish desire, man is inclined to imagine he possesses something which he actually does not, solely for the purpose of having his wishes fulfilled.

Selfishness takes the lead, and dulls the truly *pure* volition! Man will never admit this to himself, but simply allows himself to drift along. And when he can no longer persuade himself otherwise, he describes this often very obvious attempt to satisfy his questionable selfish desires as a decree of fate to which one must submit.

Therefore to guide and support him he needs still other hints which will let him experience and recognise what in truth chastity *is* as it lies in the Will of God, Who does not want any separation from nature on earth.

In the Divine Sphere Purity is closely united with Love! Hence if he is to derive blessing from them, man must not try to separate the two on earth either.

But on earth love is also no more than an evil caricature of what it *really* is. Thus unless it first undergoes a change it cannot unite with the true concept of purity.

To all those who strive to attain chastity, I herewith give a hint which provides the support that man needs on earth in order to live *in such a way* as rests in the Law of Creation, and as is therefore also pleasing to God:

"He who in his actions always remembers not to harm his fellow-man who reposes trust in him, not to do anything that may later oppress him, will always act *in such a way* as to remain spiritually unburdened, and may therefore be called truly chaste!"

These simple words, rightly understood, can fully protect and guide man through the entire Creation, and lead him upwards into the Luminous Gardens, his true home. These words are the key to all rightful activity on earth; for genuine chastity lies in them.

The Son of God Jesus expressed precisely the same in the words: "Love thy neighbour as thyself!"

But you must beware of falling back into the old human faults, and of once more construing and partly distorting the meaning of the words so as to make them serve your own purpose, soothe you in your wrong-doing, and lull your fellow-men into carelessness or even help to mislead them.

Absorb such words as they are truly meant to be absorbed, not as appears convenient to you and suits your stubborn volition. Then for you they will be like the keenest sword in your hand, with which you can slay all Darkness if you but will. Let them become alive within you in the right way so that, filled with gratitude, you may grasp life on earth as jubilant victors!

THE FIRST STEP

LET MY Word become *alive* within you; for *this* alone can bring you *that* benefit which you need, enabling your spirit to ascend to the Luminous Heights of the Eternal Gardens of God.

It is of no avail to *know* of the Word! And if you could recite my entire Message sentence by sentence from memory, in order to teach yourselves and your fellow-men ... it is of no avail unless you *act* accordingly, *think* in the sense of my Word, and adjust your whole earth-life to it as a matter of course, as something which has become an integral part of your being, which cannot be separated from you. Only then will you be able to draw from my Message the eternal values it holds for you.

"By their *works* ye shall know them!" This saying of Christ is *primarily* intended for all the readers of my Message! By their works means by their *activity,* that is, by their thinking and deeds in their daily life on earth! Your deeds also include your speech, not only your actions; for speaking *is* action, the effect of which you have hitherto under-estimated. Even your *thoughts* are included here.

Men are in the habit of saying that thoughts are "free". By this they wish to imply that they cannot be held accountable on earth for their thoughts, because these are on a level which is inaccessible to human hands.

Therefore they often *play* with thoughts in the most careless way or, better expressed, they play *in* thoughts. Unfortunately often a very dangerous game, in the light-hearted illusion that they can emerge from it unharmed.

But here they err; for thoughts too belong to the *World of Gross Matter,* and must in all circumstances also be redeemed in it before a spirit becomes capable of swinging itself freely upwards, once it has severed the connection with its earthly body.

Therefore seek at all times to swing even with your thoughts in the sense of my Message, in such a way that you desire only what is *noble,* and do not lower yourselves because you imagine that nobody can see or hear it.

Thoughts, words and the visible deed all belong to the Realm of Gross Matter in this Creation!

Thoughts operate in the World of *Fine* Gross Matter, words in the World of *Medium* Gross Matter, and visible actions take form in the World of *coarsest,* that is, *densest* Gross Matter. These three kinds of your activity are *gross material!*

But the forms of all three are closely connected with each other, their effects are interwoven. What that implies for you, how incisive and decisive its effect often is in the course of your existence, you cannot estimate all at once.

It means nothing else than that also a thought, automatically working on according to its nature, can strengthen a homogeneous type in the World of *Medium* Matter, thereby producing more powerful forms; likewise then, deducing from this, it again continues to work on within this intensification, and arises in a visible active form in the *coarsest* World of Matter, without you yourselves seeming to be directly concerned with it.

It comes as a shock to know this, when one realises how superficial and careless these earthmen are in their thinking.

Thus without knowing it you *participate* in many a deed perpetrated by one or other of your fellow-men, simply because he has received the intensification in the way I have just explained to you. It became capable of driving him to the crudest perpetration of something that had hitherto slumbered within him, with which previously he had always merely toyed in his thoughts.

Thus many a person on earth very often looks with disapproval upon some action of one of his fellow-men, angrily repudiating and condemning it, and yet he is *partially responsible* for it before the Eternal Laws of God! In this someone who is a complete stranger to him may be involved, and it may concern a deed which he himself would never have committed in the Realm of Coarsest Matter.

Think yourselves deeply into such happenings for once, and you will then all the more understand why I call to you in my Message: *"Keep the hearth of your thoughts pure, by so doing you will bring peace and be happy!"*

But when you have become sufficiently strong in this respect through your own purification, far fewer crimes than hitherto, in which many have been unknowingly implicated, will be committed on earth.

The time and place of such deeds as you may become implicated in are of no importance here. Even if they occurred at the opposite end of the earth to where you live, in places where you have never set foot, of whose existence you have no knowledge whatever. Through your toying with thoughts intensifications will strike *wherever* they discover homogeneous types, independent of distances, nation and country.

Thus in the course of time thoughts of hate and envy may thrust themselves upon individuals, groups or whole nations, wherever they find homogeneity, impelling them to actions expressed in forms entirely different from those that first arose through your toying with thoughts.

The final result may then manifest according to the inner state of the *perpetrator* at the time of the deed. Thus you may have contributed to the perpetration of such horrible deeds as you yourselves have never really contemplated, and yet you are connected with them, and a part of the reaction must burden your spirit, must hang on it like a weight when it severs itself from the body.

But on the other hand you can also contribute even more powerfully to the peace and happiness of humanity, and through pure, joyful thinking can have a share in works that develop through total strangers.

From this the blessing also naturally flows back to you, and you do not realise why.

If you could but once *see* how the immutable Justice of God's All-Holy Will is always fulfilled in the self-acting Laws of this Creation for every single thought you harbour, you would strive with all your might to attain purity in your thinking!

Only then will you have become *such* human beings as the Creator in His Work will mercifully guide to the knowledge that bestows eternal life upon them, allowing them to become helpers in Creation worthy to receive the high blessings destined for the human spirit; so that these may be joyfully and gratefully transformed and passed on to *those* creatures who are only able to absorb them through such a transformation by man, and who today, through the decline of the human spirit, remain wantonly cut off from them, after it had already been possible for them to come into existence in times of a better and more purely swinging humanity.

With this, however, you will have made only *one* sentence from my Message glow with vitality for yourselves on earth!

For you it is the *most difficult one,* which will then make all the rest much easier, whose fulfilment must already let miracle upon miracle arise before you in earthly *visible* and tangible form. –

When you have conquered yourselves *in this,* you will be confronted on your path with yet another danger resulting from the distortion of human thinking: You will recognise in it a power which you will wish to press all too readily into quite definite forms, so that it may serve this or that special purpose made up of selfish desires!

Already today I wish to *warn* you against this; for the danger can engulf you, you would perish in it, even after you have set out on the right path.

Beware of a *desperate struggle* to enforce this purity of thoughts; for in so doing you would already press them into definite channels, and your effort would become an illusion, would always be only *artificially* enforced, and could never have the great effect that it should have. Your efforts would bring harm rather than benefit, because they lack the genuineness of the free intuition. Again it would be a product of your *intellectual volition,* but never the work of your spirit! Against this I warn you.

Remember my Word of the Message which tells you that all true greatness can lie only in *simplicity,* since true greatness *is* simple! You may be better able to understand *that* simplicity which I mean here, if for the time being you use instead the human-earthly concept of *being unassuming.* This perhaps comes nearer to your comprehension, and you will hit upon the true meaning.

You cannot give the purity that I mean to your thoughts through your thought-volition; but the pure volition, *unassuming* and boundless, must well up within you from your intuitive perception, not compressed into a word which can only give rise to a limited concept. That must not be; but an all-embracing urge for the good, able to envelop your thoughts as they arise and to permeate them even before they take form, is the right thing which you need.

It is not difficult, indeed much easier than the other attempts, once you become unassuming, whereby intellectual conceit about your own abilities and your own power cannot arise. Empty yourselves of thoughts, and set free within you the urge for what is noble and good. Then you will have *that* foundation for thinking which comes from the volition of your *spirit;* and whatever arises *from that* you can then safely leave to the work of your intellect to carry out in the Realm of Densest Gross Matter. Nothing wrong can ever develop.

Cast off all the torment caused by thoughts, and trust instead in your *spirit*, which will surely find the right way if you yourselves do not wall it up. Become *free in spirit*, which means nothing else than *let the spirit within you have its way!* Then it simply *cannot* do other than journey towards the height; for its very nature draws it upwards with all certainty. Hitherto you have restrained it so that it could no longer unfold, thereby you had restricted its flight or bound its wings.

The foundation for the upbuilding of a new humanity, which you cannot and must not evade, rests in the one sentence: *Keep the hearth of your thoughts pure!*

And it is *with this* that man must begin! That is his *first* task which will make him *what* he *must* become. An *example* to all who strive for Light and Truth, who wish to serve the Creator gratefully through the nature of their whole being. He who fulfils *this* needs no further directions. He *is* as he should be, and will thus receive the full measure of help that awaits him in Creation and leads him upwards without interruption.

THE WORLD

The World! When man uses this word he often utters it thoughtlessly, without forming a picture of *what* this world he speaks of is really *like*.

Many, however, who try to picture something definite visualise countless celestial bodies of the most varied nature and size arranged in solar systems, pursuing their courses in the Universe. They know that ever new and more celestial bodies can be seen as stronger and more far-reaching instruments are produced. The average man is then satisfied with the word "infinity", and thereby the error of a *wrong* conception sets in with him.

The World is not infinite. It is the material Creation, that is, the *Work* of the Creator. This Work, like every work, stands *beside* the Creator, and as such is finite.

So-called advanced thinkers often pride themselves on having the recognition that God rests in all Creation, in every flower, every stone; that the driving forces of nature are God, thus everything that is beyond investigation, what is sensed but cannot really be grasped. An ever-active Primordial Energy, the Source of Power, Itself eternally evolving anew, the Unsubstantiate Primordial Light. They consider themselves mightily advanced in the consciousness of finding God everywhere, of encountering Him everywhere, as an all-pervading driving Power, ever working towards the one goal of further development to perfection.

But only in a certain sense is this true. What we encounter in all Creation is only His Will and thus His Spirit, His Power. He Himself stands far above Creation.

From its very inception the Material Creation was bound to the unalterable Laws of evolution and dissolution; for what we call the Laws of Nature are the Creative Will of God, which in its activity is continually forming and dissolving worlds. This Creative Will is *uniform* in all Creation, to which the Ethereal World and the Gross Material World belong as *one*.

The absolute and immutable uniformity of the Primordial Laws, thus of the Primordial Will, ordains that in the most minute process of the gross material earth the course is always exactly the same as it must be in every happening, thus also in the most stupendous events of the entire Creation, and in the creative process itself.

The strict form of the Primordial Will is plain and simple. Once it is recognised we easily discover it in everything. The complexity and incomprehensibility of many happenings lies solely in the manifold interlacing of the detours and by-paths formed by the varied volitions of men.

Thus the Work of God, the World, is as Creation subject to the Divine Laws, which are constant in all things and perfect; it also issued from them, and is therefore finite.

The artist, for example, also is in his work, merges with it, and yet personally stands beside it. The work is limited and transient, but not the talent of the artist on that account. The artist, that is, the creator of the work, can destroy his work, in which lies his volition, without himself being affected by it. Nevertheless he will still remain the artist.

We recognise and discern the artist in his work, and he becomes familiar to us without our needing to see him personally. We have his works, his volition lies in them and influences us, he confronts us in them, and yet may himself be living his own life far away from us.

The creative artist and his work faintly reflect the relation of the Creation to the Creator.

It is only the *cycle* of Creation, in its continuous coming into being, disintegration and re-formation, that is eternal and without end, thus infinite.

All the revelations and prophecies, too, are fulfilled within this happening. Finally the "Last Judgment" for the earth will also be fulfilled in it!

The Last, that is, the *Final* Judgment, comes one day for *each* material celestial globe, but it does not take place simultaneously in the whole of Creation.

It is a process necessary in that particular part of Creation which reaches the point in its cycle where its disintegration must set in, so that it can form itself anew on its further course.

This eternal cycle does not refer to the orbit of the earth and other stars around their suns, but to the great and mightier cycle which must in turn be followed by all the solar systems, while they in themselves also carry out their own movements separately.

Again, by reason of the consistency of the Natural Laws, the point at which disintegration of each celestial globe must begin is precisely determined. A very definite place at which the process of disintegration *must* develop, irrespective of the condition of the celestial globe concerned and of its inhabitants.

The cycle drives every celestial globe irresistibly towards this point, the hour of disintegration will be fulfilled without delay; as with everything in Creation this actually denotes only a transformation, the opportunity for a further development. Then the hour of the "either – or" has come for every human being. Either he is raised high towards the Light if he strives for the spiritual, or he remains chained to the World of Matter, to which he clings if out of conviction he declares that only material things are of value.

In that case, through the lawful consequence of his own volition, he is unable to rise from the World of Matter, and on the last stretch of the way he is drawn with it into disintegration. This then is spiritual death! Equivalent to effacement from the Book of Life.

This process, in itself quite natural, is also designated as eternal damnation, because he who is thus drawn along into disintegration "must cease to be personal". It is the most dreadful thing that can befall man. He is considered as a "rejected stone", which cannot be used for a spiritual building and must therefore be ground to dust.

This separation of spirit from matter, likewise taking place by reason of quite natural processes and Laws is the so-called "Last Judgment", which is connected with great upheavals and transformations.

Surely everyone will readily understand that this disintegration will not take place in *one* earth day; for in world events a thousand years are as one day.

But we are well into the early stages of this epoch. The earth now approaches the point at which it diverges from its hitherto existing course, which must also make itself strongly felt in gross matter. Then the separation among all men, which has already been prepared for some time, but which until now has only manifested itself in "opinions and convictions", will set in more sharply.

Every hour of an earth-life is therefore more precious than ever. He who earnestly seeks, and is willing to learn, should exert all his strength to tear himself from base thoughts, which must chain him to earthly things. Otherwise he is in danger of remaining attached to the World of Matter, and being drawn with it towards complete disintegration.

Those who strive for the Light, however, will gradually become detached from the World of Matter, and will finally be uplifted to the home of all that is spiritual.

Then the division between Light and Darkness will be finally accomplished, and the Judgment fulfilled.

It is not "the World", that is to say all Creation, which will perish thereby, but the celestial globes will only be drawn into the disintegrating process when their course reaches the point where dissolution, and with it also the preceding separation, is due to set in.

This is accomplished through the natural effect of the Divine Laws, which have lain in Creation from its very beginnings, which brought forth Creation itself, and which also now and in the future unswervingly bear the Will of the Creator. In the eternal cycle there is a perpetual creating, sowing, ripening, harvesting and dissolving, so that, newly invigorated through the change in the combination, other forms may again evolve, speeding towards a new cycle.

In considering this cycle of Creation, one may picture a gigantic funnel or a gigantic cave, from which in an incessant stream there perpetually gushes forth primordial seed, striving in rotating movements towards fresh union and development. Exactly as science already knows and has correctly noted.

Through friction and amalgamation dense nebulae are formed, and from these again celestial globes, which through immutable Laws group themselves with absolute consistency into solar systems; and rotating individually, they must unitedly follow the great cycle which is the eternal one.

Exactly as it is in the process that is visible to the physical eye in connection with plant, animal and human bodies, where there ensue from the seed the development, forming, maturity and harvest or decay, thus entailing a change, a disintegration, leading to further development, so is it also in great world events. The gross materially visible celestial globes, surrounded as they are by a far greater ethereal environment that is therefore invisible to the physical eye, are subject to the same process in their eternal cycle, because the same Laws are active in them.

Not even the most fanatical sceptic is able to deny the existence of primordial seed, and yet it cannot be seen by any physical eye because it is of a different substance which lies in the "beyond". Let us again simply call it ethereal.

Nor is it difficult to understand that in the natural order of things the world that *first* forms itself from primordial seed is equally ethereal, and not discernible with the physical eyes. Only *later* the *coarsest* precipitation further resulting from it gradually forms, dependent on the Ethereal World, the Gross Material World with its gross material bodies; and it is *only that* which can be observed from its minutest beginnings with the physical eyes and with all additional gross material aids.

It is no different with the covering of the real man in his spiritual nature, of whom I shall yet speak later. During his wanderings through the various worlds his garment, cloak, shell, body or instrument, no matter what one cares to call the covering, must always be of the same substance as the particular environment which he enters, so that he can make use of it as a protection and necessary aid if he wishes to be able to work *directly* and effectively therein.

Since the Gross Material World is dependent upon the Ethereal World, it follows that whatever happens in the Gross Material World also reacts on the Ethereal World.

This immense ethereal environment has likewise been created from the primordial seed. It takes part in the eternal cycle, and is finally also driven towards and sucked into the rear end of the aforesaid gigantic funnel, where disintegration takes place, in order to be thrust out again at the other end as primordial seed for a new cycle.

As with the action of the heart and the blood circulation, the funnel is like the heart of material creation. Thus the process of disintegration involves the whole of Creation, including the ethereal part, because *everything* that is material is again dissolved into primordial seed in order to form itself anew. There is nothing arbitrary in this, but everything develops out of the natural consistency of the Primordial Laws, which permit of no other course.

Hence at a certain point of the great cycle the moment arrives for all that is created, whether gross material or ethereal, when the process of disintegration is prepared independently from out of what is created, and finally breaks through.

Now this Ethereal World is the transitional dwelling-place of the earthly departed, the so-called beyond. It is closely connected with the Gross Material World, which is part of it and one with it. At the moment of death man, with his ethereal body, which he bears along with the gross material body, enters the homogeneous ethereal environment of the Gross Material World, while he leaves the gross material body behind on the latter.

Now this Ethereal World, the beyond, belonging as it does to Creation, is subject to the same Laws of continuous development and disintegration. With the setting-in of decay, a separation of the spiritual from the material again takes place in a perfectly natural way. According to man's spiritual state in the Gross Material World as well as in the Ethereal World, the spiritual man, the real "ego", must either move upwards or remain chained to the World of Matter.

The serious longing for Truth and Light will, by virtue of the change it works in him, make each person spiritually purer and thus more luminous, so that this condition must naturally detach him more and more from dense matter, and drive him upwards in proportion to his purity and lightness.

However, he who believes only in matter keeps himself bound to matter by his conviction, remaining chained to it, and thus cannot be driven upwards. Through a decision personally desired by each individual, a separation therefore takes place between those striving towards the Light and those connected with the Darkness, in accordance with the existing natural Laws of Spiritual Gravitation.

Thus it becomes clear that one day there will be a *definite end* also to the possibility of development through the purification-process in the so-called beyond for those who have departed this earth. A final decision! Men in both worlds will either be so far ennobled that they can be uplifted to the Regions of Light, or they will remain bound in their base nature through their own volition and thereby be finally hurled down into "eternal damnation". This means that together with matter, from which they cannot detach themselves, they will be drawn towards disintegration, will themselves suffer painful disintegration, and therewith cease to be personal.

They will be scattered like chaff in the wind, crumbled to dust and thereby erased from the Golden Book of Life!

Hence this so-called "Last Judgment", that is, the Final Judgment, is likewise a happening which through the operation of the Laws upholding Creation takes place in an absolutely natural manner, and in such a way that it could not be otherwise. Here, too, man always receives only the fruits of what he himself has willed, that is to say, what he himself brings about through his conviction.

It does not diminish the greatness of the Creator, but can only give cause to regard Him as even more sublime, to know that all that happens in Creation is strictly consistent and takes place automatically, that the direction of men's fate is always determined by themselves alone through their wishes and volition, and that the Creator does not look on and intervene to reward or punish.

The greatness lies in the *perfection* of His Work, and this compels us to look upwards in reverential awe, since the greatest Love and the most incorruptible Justice must lie without distinction in the mightiest as well as in the most minute happening.

Great also is man, placed as such in Creation as master of his own destiny! Through his will he is able to lift himself out of the Work, and at the same time contribute to its higher evolution; or he can drag it down and become entangled in it so that he can no longer free himself and will continue with it towards dissolution, whether in the Gross Material World or in the Ethereal World.

Therefore strive to free yourselves from all ties arising from base feelings; for it is high time! The hour approaches when the period allotted for this will have expired! Awake in yourselves the longing for the pure, the true and the noble! –

Far above the eternal cycle of Creation there floats like a crown in the centre an "Azure Island", the abode of the blessed, of the purified spirits, who may already dwell in the Regions of Light! This Island is separate from the World. Therefore it has no part in the cycle; but in spite of its height above the rotating Creation, it constitutes the support and the centre for the outgoing spiritual forces. It is the island that bears on its height the muchpraised city with its streets of gold. Here nothing is subject any longer to change. No "Last Judgment" is to be feared any more. Those who can dwell there are "at home".

But as the last, as the highest on this Azure Island, inaccessible to those not specially called, stands the ... Grail Castle, so often spoken of in poetry!

Encompassed by legends, the object of longing to so many, it stands there in the Light of Greatest Glory and harbours the Sacred Vessel of the Pure Love of the Almighty, the Grail!

The purest of spirits are appointed as guardians. They are bearers of Divine Love in its purest form, which is very different from what men on earth imagine it to be, although they experience it daily and hourly.

Through revelations, tidings of the Castle were brought down stage by stage the immense distance from the Azure Island through the Ethereal World, until finally, through a few deeply inspired poets, they also became known among people of the gross material earth. Passed on downwards step by step, the Truth also unintentionally suffered various misrepresentations, so that the final version could only be an increasingly dimmed reflection, which gave rise to many errors.

If now from some part of the great Creation in dire distress, suffering and ardent appeals rise to the Creator, then a Servant of the Vessel is sent forth as a bearer of this Love to intervene helpingly in the spiritual need. What floats merely as a myth and a legend in the Work of Creation then enters Creation as a living reality!

Such missions, however, do not often occur. Each time they are accompanied by incisive changes and great upheavals. Those who are thus sent bring Light and Truth to the erring, Peace to the despairing; with their message they stretch forth their hands to all who seek, offering them new courage and new strength, and guiding them through all Darkness up to the Light.

They come only for those who long for help from the Light, but not for the scoffers and the self-righteous.

THE STAR OF BETHLEHEM

THERE shall now be Light here on earth, as once it should have been when the Star of Promise shone radiantly above a stable in Bethlehem.

But at that time only a few accepted the Light, and those who listened to them very soon distorted and misrepresented it, as men on earth are apt to do. What they forgot they tried to replace with ideas of their own, thereby creating only a confusion that nowadays is meant to pass as inviolable Truth.

Out of alarm that everything will collapse if even the smallest pillar proves to be unsound, every ray of Light that can bring recognition is resisted, defiled and, if there is no other way, at least ridiculed with a malice and cunning which plainly indicates to clear thinking that it springs from fear! But clear thinking is only rarely to be found on earth.

In spite of this the light of true recognition *must* at last come over all mankind!

The time has arrived when everything unhealthy invented by the human brain will be swept out of Creation, so that it no longer suppresses the enlightenment that the Truth wears a *different* aspect from the unsteady images which boastful conceit and commercialism, morbid imagination and hypocrisy, in a craving for earthly power and earthly admiration, have created out of the sultry swamp of base narrow-mindedness.

Accursed now be those who through leading millions of people astray have so enslaved them that today they no longer dare to open their eyes to the Light, but blindly revile anything coming to their knowledge that sounds different from what they have hitherto heard, instead of at last listening attentively and examining inwardly to see whether the new does not come nearer to their understanding than what they have learned in the past.

Their ears are stopped, and anxiously they see to it that no breath of fresh air penetrates to them. Actually just out of laziness and fear that this fresh air, through the ensuing recovery, implies *spiritual activity*, demanding and enforcing self-exertion. In contrast to the present apparently comfortable spiritual slumber, which is followed by the heavy permanent sleep, and thereby only gives a free hand to the cunning of the distorted, debased intellect!

But it is of no avail to stop your ears against the new Word, to shut your eyes lest the Light dazzle and startle you! You will now be *forcibly* roused from this deplorable stupor! You will have to stand shivering before the cold Light that mercilessly strips you of all false wrappings. Shivering because your spirit-spark can no longer be kindled *within you,* and thus generate the warmth from within that will unite with the Light.

Indeed it is all too *easy* for you to *believe* the *unbelievable;* for then you need not trouble to think and examine for yourselves. Just because it cannot stand up to any test that is in accordance with the Divine Laws of Nature, you simply *have* to believe, without questioning the why or wherefore; you have to believe *blindly,* and this you imagine to be *great!* You who so conveniently imagine you are particularly devout, simply raise yourselves above all doubts in this matter, and ... feel happy, secure, noble, pious and sure of a place in Heaven!

However, you have not thereby raised yourselves above all doubt, but only bypassed it in a cowardly way! You were too spiritually indolent to bestir yourselves, and preferred blind faith to a knowledge of the natural happening in the Law of God's Will. Fictions devised by the human brain aided you in this. For the more absurd and incomprehensible the things you are supposed to believe, the easier it also becomes literally to believe in them *blindly,* because in such matters it is quite impossible to do otherwise. Knowledge and conviction *must* be eliminated then.

Only the impossible demands blind, unreserved faith; for whatever is possible immediately stimulates independent thinking. Wherever there is Truth, which is always characterised by naturalness and consistency, thinking and deep intuitive sensing automatically set in. This only ceases where it no longer finds anything natural, thus where Truth does not exist. And it is *only* through deep intuitive sensing that anything can become conviction, which alone brings values to the human spirit.

So now, along with everything else, the cycle which begins with the Holy Night in Bethlehem is also closing! And the closing of this cycle must cast out all inaccuracies in the transmissions, and in their stead bring the Truth to victory. The Darkness created by humanity is dispelled by the penetrating Light!

All legends which in the course of time have been woven around the life of Jesus must fall away so that it may at last emerge in purity, in accordance with Divine Laws, as indeed it could not have been otherwise in this Creation. Hitherto you have credulously and wantonly denied the Perfection of the Creator, your God, with your self-established cults.

You deliberately and consciously represent Him in these cults as imperfect in His Will! I have already spoken about this and, turn and twist as you will, not a *single* subterfuge can acquit you of having been too indolent to think about it yourselves. You do not honour God by blindly believing in things that are not in accordance with the Primordial Laws of Creation! On the contrary, if you believe in the Perfection of the Creator, then you must know that nothing can happen here in Creation that does not also precisely conform to the logical sequence in the firmly established Laws of God. Only therein can you truly honour Him.

He who thinks otherwise thus doubts the *Perfection* of the Creator, his God! For where alterations or further improvements are possible, there is not and never has been perfection! Development is something different. This is provided for and intended in this Creation. However, it must follow unconditionally *as a logical sequence* of the effect of already existing Laws. But all this cannot produce such things as many believers take for granted, especially in the life of Christ!

Wake up from your dreams at last and become inwardly *true!* Let it be said once more that according to the Laws in Creation it is impossible for bodies of earthmen ever to be born without previous physical procreation, and equally impossible for a physical body to be raised into the Ethereal Realm after its earthly death, still less into the Animistic or even the Spiritual Realm! And since Jesus had to be born here on earth, this event was also subject to the gross material Divine Law of a previous procreation.

If it had happened with Christ as transmissions report, God would have to act against His own Laws. But this He cannot do since He is *perfect from the very beginning*, and thus also His Will, Which lies in the Laws of Creation. Whoever still dares to think otherwise doubts this Perfection and thus ultimately also doubts God! For God without Perfection would not be God. There can be no subterfuge! No human spirit can quibble about this simple certainty, even if the foundations of many a former opinion must now be shaken thereby. Here there is only either – or. All or nothing. There can be no compromise, because nothing incomplete or unfinished can exist in the Godhead! Nor in anything concerned with God!

Jesus was procreated *physically*, otherwise an earthly birth would not have been possible.

At that time only a few recognised the Star as the fulfilment of the prophecies. Among them were Mary herself, and also Joseph who, deeply stirred, hid his face.

Three kings found their way to the stable and presented earthly gifts; but then they went away, leaving without protection the Child Whose earthly path they should have smoothed with their wealth and power, so that no harm might befall Him in the fulfilment of His Mission. Although they received enlightenment enabling them to find the Child, they did not fully recognise their sublime call.

Disquietude drove Mary away from Nazareth, and Joseph, seeing her silent suffering and longing, granted her wish solely to make her happy. He handed over the management of his carpenter's shop to his oldest employee, and with Mary and the Child journeyed to a distant country. In the course of their everyday life of work and cares, the memory of the Radiant Star slowly faded from their minds, especially as in His early years Jesus displayed nothing extraordinary, but like all children was quite natural.

It was only on his deathbed, after returning to his native town, that Joseph, who had always been the best of fatherly friends to Jesus, saw in his passing, during his last moments on earth, the Cross and the Dove above Jesus, Who stood alone at his bedside. Deeply stirring were his last words: "So Thou art He after all!"

Jesus Himself knew nothing of this until something urged Him to go to John, of whom He had heard that he was proclaiming wise teachings and baptising at the River Jordan.

With this gross material act of baptism, the beginning of the Mission was firmly anchored in the World of Gross Matter. The bandage fell. From this moment Jesus Himself was conscious that He was to carry the Word of the Father among mankind on earth.

His whole life as it really was will unfold itself before you, divested of all the fantasies invented by human brains! With the closing of the cycle of this event, it will be revealed to all during the Judgment through the victory of the Truth, which for a long time to come may no longer be obscured!

Mary fought an inward battle with her doubts, which were strengthened through motherly anxiety for her son, right up to the grievous walk to Golgotha. Purely human and not supernatural. Only there did recognition of His Mission, and with it belief, finally come to her.

But now, at the return of the Star, all errors shall henceforth be redeemed through the Grace of God; and likewise all the faults of those who, without obstinacy or evil intent, rendered Christ's way more difficult at that time; and who now at the closing of the cycle come to recognition, and try to make good their neglect or failures.

Through their desire to make good, redemption arises for them with the Radiant Star; liberated, they can give jubilant thanks to Him Who in His Wisdom and Goodness created the Laws by which all creatures must judge and also redeem themselves.

THE CONFLICT

Up till now there could be no question as yet of a sharp confrontation between two world views. Conflict is therefore an ill-chosen term for what is actually happening between the intellectuals and serious seekers for the Truth.

All that has so far taken place has consisted of one-sided attacks by the intellectuals, which to any dispassionate observer must appear obviously unfounded and often absurd. Scorn, hostility, and even persecution of a most serious kind await all those who seek to develop themselves higher in a purely spiritual sense, even when they maintain silent reserve. There are always some who try by ridicule or force to pull back and drag down such aspiring ones to the dull insensibility or hypocrisy of the masses.

Thus many were bound to become actual martyrs, because not only the masses but therewith also the earthly power has been on the side of the intellectuals. What these have to offer is already clearly indicated in the word "intellect". That is: A narrowing of the range of the perceptive capacity to purely earthly matters, and thus to the minutest part of real existence.

It is easily understandable that this can produce nothing perfect, nothing good whatever for a humanity whose existence moves mainly through spheres which the intellectuals have closed to themselves. Especially so when one considers that just one brief earth-life should become a significant turning-point for the whole existence, entailing as it does decisive interventions in those other spheres which are completely inconceivable to the intellectuals.

The responsibility of the intellectuals, who rightly considered have already fallen deeply, is thus enormously increased, and as heavy pressure it will help to push them more and more swiftly towards the goal of their choice, so that they will at last have to partake of the fruits of what they have persistently and presumptuously advocated.

By intellectuals are to be understood those who have unconditionally submitted themselves to their own intellect. These people, strange to say, have for thousands of years believed that they had an absolute right to impose their limited convictions by law and by force also upon those who wished to live according to another conviction. This utterly illogical presumption again lies only in the intellectuals' narrow perceptive capacity, which is incapable of lifting itself higher. This very limitation brings them a so-called peak of comprehension, whereby such presumptions are bound to arise in the imagination, because they believe they really are standing on the utmost height. This is actually true so far as they are concerned, since they have arrived at the boundary which they cannot cross.

But their attacks on seekers for the Truth, so often inexplicably malevolent, clearly show on closer observation the whip of the Darkness brandished behind them. Seldom does one find in these hostile acts a trace of honest volition, which might somewhat excuse their often shocking manner of proceeding. In most cases there is only blind fury devoid of any real logic. Just examine such attacks dispassionately. How seldom is there among them an article whose contents indicate an attempt to enter really *objectively* into the speeches or essays of a seeker for the Truth.

The unfounded and paltry nature of the attacks is always quite strikingly apparent from the very fact that these are *never kept purely objective!* They are always a veiled or open defilement of the *person* of the Truth-seeker. *This is only done by someone who is incapable of replying objectively.* After all, a seeker for the Truth or a bringer of the Truth does not give himself *personally*, but he brings what he *says*.

The word must be examined, not the *person!* It is a habit of the intellectuals to seek always to regard the person first, and then to consider whether they can listen to his words. Owing to the narrow limitation of their perceptive capacity, these people *need* such an outward hold, because they must cling to externals to prevent them from becoming confused. Indeed just this is the hollow structure which they erect, which is inadequate for men and a great hindrance to their advancement.

If they had a firm inner hold they would simply let fact speak against fact, excluding the personal element altogether. But this they are unable to do. Indeed, they intentionally avoid it because they feel or partly know that in a well-ordered tournament they would be quickly unseated. The ironic reference to "lay preacher" or "lay interpretation", so often used, shows such a degree of ridiculous presumption that every serious person immediately senses: "This is a shield used to conceal shallowness at all costs. To cover their emptiness with a cheap signboard!"

Clumsy strategy which cannot last for long. Its purpose is from the beginning to place seekers for the Truth who may become troublesome on an "inferior" if not even a ridiculous level in the eyes of their fellow-men, or at least to classify them as "dabblers" so that they will not be taken seriously.

In so doing they seek to prevent anyone from seriously paying attention to the words. The motive for this proceeding, however, is not anxiety lest their fellow-men be delayed in their inner ascent through erroneous teachings, rather it is a vague apprehension of losing influence and thereby being compelled to penetrate more deeply than before, and having to change much that till now was supposed to be unassailable, and which suited them.

It is just this frequent reference to "laymen", this strange looking down upon those who through their strengthened and less influenced intuitive perception stand much nearer to the Truth, and who have not built walls for themselves through rigid intellectual forms, that exposes a weakness whose dangers cannot escape the notice of any thinker. *He who believes in such opinions is at the outset excluded from being an unprejudiced teacher and guide,* for he stands much further away from God and His Activity than any other man.

Knowledge about the development of religions, with all the errors and faults, does not bring men nearer to their God, and just as little does the intellectual interpretation of the Bible or of other valuable writings of the different religions.

The intellect is and remains bound to time and space, that is to say earthbound; whereas the Godhead, and thus also the recognition of God and His Will, are above time and space and above all that is transitory, and therefore can never be grasped by the narrowly-confined intellect.

For this simple reason the intellect is not called upon to bring enlightenment in eternal values. Indeed it would be a contradiction. Therefore he who in *these* matters boasts of university qualifications, and would look down upon those who are not so influenced, thereby declares his own incompetence and limitation. Thinking people will at once sense intuitively the one-sidedness, and use caution against him who cautions them in such a manner!

Only those who are called can be true teachers. Called ones are those who carry the ability within them. These abilities, however, do not ask for university training, but for the vibrations of a refined intuitive faculty, able to soar above time and space, thus beyond the limit of comprehension by the earthly intellect.

Moreover, any inwardly free man will always assess a matter or a teaching according to *what* it brings, not according to *who* brings it. The latter is the strongest possible evidence of his unfitness to be an investigator. Gold is gold, whether a prince or a beggar holds it in his hand.

But just in the most valuable things of the spiritual man, one seeks obstinately to disregard and to alter this irrefutable fact. Naturally without any more success than in the case of gold. For those who are really seeking seriously do not permit themselves to be influenced by such distractions from examining the matter itself. But those who do allow themselves to be so influenced are not yet mature to receive the Truth. It is not for them.

But the hour is not far distant when a conflict, which has been lacking as yet, must now break out. The one-sidedness will end, and a sharp confrontation will follow which will destroy all false presumption.

MODERN psychic science! What gathers beneath this flag! What comes together there, and what also opposes each other beneath it! A playground for earnest seeking, little knowledge, great plans, vanity and stupidity; in many cases also for empty boasting, and still more for the most unscrupulous commercialism. Out of this confusion there frequently blossom envy and boundless hatred, which finally results in the basest kind of malicious vindictiveness.

In such a state of affairs it is naturally not surprising if many people shun all these strange activities, fearing to poison themselves by coming into contact with them. They are not far wrong either; for countless adherents of psychic science are anything but engaging in their behaviour, still less attractive; on the contrary, everything about them warns others to exercise the greatest caution.

It is strange that the whole field of so-called psychic science, which is often confused by the malicious or ignorant with *ghost* science, is today still considered a sort of *free territory* where everyone may go on in his own way and get up to his tricks unhindered, even unrestrained and unpunished.

Such is it *considered* to be. But already experiences have very often taught that it is *not* so!

Countless pioneers in this field who were rash enough to venture a few steps forward in their investigations, equipped with only an imagined knowledge, have become helpless victims of their carelessness. The only sad thing about this is that all these victims fell without bringing even the slightest benefit to humanity thereby!

Now each of these cases should really have proved that the way followed is not the right one, because it brings only harm and even destruction, but no blessing. Yet with singular persistence these false ways are still retained, and fresh victims continually sacrificed; a great clamour is raised over every small detail that is discovered and newly recognised, although self-evident in the mighty Creation, and innumerable treatises are written which must repel many serious seekers, because the uncertain groping therein is clearly perceptible.

All investigations until now can really rather be called dangerous pastimes, based on good intentions.

The field of psychic science, which is considered free territory, can never be entered upon with impunity as long as one does not *first* know how to take into account the *spiritual* Laws to their full extent. Every conscious or unconscious opposition to these Laws, that is "non-observance" of them, which is equivalent to a transgression, must through its inevitable reciprocal action strike the bold, frivolous or careless person who does not or cannot pay close attention to them.

Trying to explore the non-earthly with earthly means and possibilities is no different from placing and leaving an undeveloped child, as yet unfamiliar with earthly dangers, alone in a virgin forest, where only a man adequately equipped for it and at the height of his strength, exercising the greatest precaution, can have any prospect of surviving unharmed.

For modern psychic scientists with their present methods it is no different, even if their intentions are absolutely serious, and if they are really taking great risks for the sole purpose of gaining knowledge to help men advance across a boundary, before which they have long stood knocking and waiting.

Today these investigators still stand before it like children, helpless and groping, unaware of the dangers that may stream towards them at any moment, or pour forth through them on to others if their bungling efforts breach the natural defences, or open a door that for many had better remain closed.

As long as those desiring to forge ahead are not absolutely certain that they will be able completely and instantly to master all dangers which may arise, not only for themselves but also for others, all this can only be termed rashness, not courage.

Those "investigators" who engage in experiments act most irresponsibly of all. Attention has already been repeatedly called to the crime of hypnotism.*

Investigators experimenting in yet other ways in most cases make the regrettable mistake, knowing nothing themselves – for otherwise they would

---

* Lecture: "The Crime of Hypnotism"

surely not do it – of putting other very sensitive or mediumistic persons into either a magnetic or even a hypnotic sleep, in order to bring them nearer to the physically invisible influences of the "other world", in the hope of thereby hearing and observing various things that would not be possible if the person experimented upon was in a fully day-conscious condition.

In at least ninety-five out of a hundred cases they thus expose such persons to great dangers, which they are not yet qualified to meet; for *every kind* of artificial help towards deeper penetration is a binding of the soul, forcing it into a sensitiveness that goes further than its natural development would permit.

The result is that such a victim of experiments suddenly stands psychically in a region where he is robbed of his natural protection by the artificial help, or for which he does not have his natural protection, which can only be formed through *personal,* sound inner development.

One must picture such a pitiable person as if he stood naked, tied to a stake and pushed far out into a dangerous country as a bait, to attract and even let himself be affected by the as yet unknown life and activity there, so that he can report upon it; or so that various manifestations will also become visible to others, through his co-operation, by the giving off of certain earthly substances from his body.

A person thus experimented with is able at times, through the connection his projected soul must maintain with his earthly body, to report as through a telephone all that happens, and transmit it to the observer.

However, should the outpost thus artificially pushed forward be in some way attacked, he cannot defend himself through lack of his natural protection. He is helplessly abandoned, because with the aid of others he has been only artificially pushed into a domain where, according to the state of his own development, he either does not yet or does not at all belong. And the so-called investigator, whose thirst for knowledge pushed him into it, can do just as little to help him, since he himself is strange and inexperienced in the place whence the danger comes, and therefore unable to do anything to provide protection.

Thus it happens that the investigators unwittingly become criminals, who cannot be apprehended by earthly justice. However, this does not prevent the *spiritual* Laws from exercising their reciprocal action with full force, and chaining the investigator to his victim.

Many a person used for experiments has suffered ethereal attacks which in due course, often also quickly or immediately, have a gross-material-physical effect as well, so that physical illness or death follows, but without eliminating the harm done to the soul.

The observers who call themselves investigators, however, who push their victims into unknown regions, in most cases stand during such hazardous experiments under good earthly cover through the protection of their body and day-consciousness.

It is seldom that they share simultaneously in the dangers confronting the persons experimented with, thus that such dangers are immediately communicated to them. But then at their physical death, the transition into the Ethereal World, because they are chained to their victims they *must* inevitably go wherever these may have been drawn, so that together with them they may slowly begin to ascend once more.

The artificial projection of a soul into another domain must not always be taken to mean that the soul leaves the body and floats away to another region. In *most* cases it remains quietly in the body. But the magnetic or hypnotic sleep makes the soul unnaturally sensitive, so that it responds to much finer currents and influences than would be possible in its natural state.

It is self-evident that in this unnatural condition the full strength is not available, which the soul would otherwise possess if it had attained this point through its own inner development, and would therefore stand firmly and securely on this new and more refined soil, bringing an equal strength to bear on all influences.

Because of this lack of sound full vigour, the artificiality produces an inequality which is bound to entail disturbances. As a result all intuitive perceptions become absolutely blurred, giving rise to distortions of reality.

The cause of the false reports and countless errors is again always given only by the investigators themselves, through their harmful assistance. That is also why in the many "investigated" matters from the occult field already available so much does not accord with strict logic. They contain countless errors, which until now could not yet be recognised as such.

Absolutely nothing that could be of the slightest use or blessing to mankind is gained by these obviously wrong methods.

Actually only that which helps men *upwards*, or at least points a way thereto, can be of any use to them. But from the outset there can be absolutely no question of this as far as these experiments are concerned!

Sometimes, however, an investigator through artificial assistance may ultimately be able to crowd some sensitive or mediumistic human being out of his earthly gross material body into the Ethereal World nearest to him, but *not* a hair's breadth *above* the region to which in any case he belongs by virtue of his inner development. On the contrary, through artificial assistance he cannot even bring him that far, but always only to the environment nearest to all that is earthly.

However, this environment nearest to the earthly can only contain all that of the beyond which is still closely earthbound, which remains chained to the earth by its inferiority, its vice and passion.

Naturally, now and then something more advanced will also make a short stay in this environment. But it is not always to be expected. Something exalted cannot be there, purely by virtue of the Natural Laws. Sooner would the world be turned upside down, or ... a foundation for anchoring the Light exist in a human being!

It is hardly to be assumed, however, that this should be sought either in a person experimented upon or in such a groping investigator. Thus the danger and uselessness of all experiments remains.

Moreover it is certain that unless there is a human being of advanced development, whose presence purifies all coarseness, something really higher can *not* approach a medium, much less speak through him. Materialisations from *higher* circles are altogether out of the question, to say nothing of such popular pastimes as knocking, movements of objects, and so on. The gulf for this is far too wide to be easily bridged.

Even with a medium, all these things can only be carried out by such souls in the beyond as are still very closely connected with matter. Were it otherwise possible, that is to say, if an exalted being could so easily make contact with humanity, then there would have been no need whatever for Christ to become man, but He could have accomplished His Mission also without this sacrifice.* Men of today, however, are certainly no more highly developed psychically than in Jesus' earth-life, so it cannot be assumed that it is easier to establish a link with the Light now than it was in those days.

* Lecture: "The Redeemer"

Now psychic scientists declare, of course, that their primary aim is to establish that there is life in the beyond, and especially that life continues after physical death; and that in view of the scepticism prevailing today very strong and forceful arguments are needed, hence *earthly tangible* proofs, to breach the defences of the adversaries.

But this reasoning does not justify the repeated endangering of human souls in such a wanton way!

Besides, there is really no compelling need to set about convincing malevolent opponents at all costs! Surely it is well known that even if an angel came directly from Heaven to proclaim the Truth to them they would not be prepared to believe. As soon as he had gone they would simply affirm that it was a mass hallucination and no angel at all, or trump up some other excuse. And if any thing or any body were brought, which or who remains in an earthly state, thus neither vanishing nor becoming invisible, there would again be other excuses, just because it would then be too earthly for those who do not wish to believe in a beyond.

They would not hesitate to declare such a proof a swindle, and the person a visionary, a fanatic, or likewise a swindler. Whether it be too earthly or too unearthly, or both together, they will always have some fault to find and doubt to express. And if they know of no other way to help themselves, then they will take to abuse, proceed to even more vigorous attacks, and will not shrink from violence.

Therefore, to convince *these,* sacrifices are not called for! Still less, however, for many of the so-called adherents. With a strange kind of arrogance, due to their generally rather vague and fantastic belief in life in the beyond, these think they can make certain demands on it whereby they in turn must "see" or "experience" something. They expect signs from their guides in the beyond as a reward for their good behaviour.

The expectations they harbour, which they consider to be their natural due, are often as utterly ridiculous as the much-knowing, leniently forgiving smile with which they mask their real ignorance. It is poison to wish even to give performances to these masses; for since they imagine they know so much, the experiments are little more to them than well-earned hours of entertainment, in which those in the beyond are expected to act as music-hall artistes.

But just let us leave the big experiments now and consider the small ones, such as table-turning. These are by no means as harmless as people imagine, but because of the extreme ease with which these practices can spread they are a *very grave danger!*

Everyone should be warned against this! Enlightened persons must turn away in horror when they see how lightly these things are treated. How many adherents seek to display their "knowledge" in various circles by suggesting experiments in table-turning, or by introducing into families, with smiles or mysterious whispers, the almost playful practice with letters and a glass, or some other aid, which when the hand is lightly laid on it glides or is drawn along to various letters, thus forming words.

With uncanny rapidity all this has developed into party games carried out amid laughter, derision and at times a kind of pleasant thrill.

Every day older and younger ladies, in families or also alone, are seated at a little table before a piece of cardboard on which letters have been drawn, which if possible must even be of a very special design, so that the hocus-pocus stimulating the imagination is not lacking. Actually this is quite unnecessary; for the object would also be accomplished without it, if the person concerned has only some tendency towards these things. And those who have are innumerable!

Modern psychic scientists and leaders of occult societies are glad of this, because real words and sentences are formed of which the person practising has neither consciously nor unconsciously been thinking. He must thereby become convinced and increase the number of adherents of the "occult".

Publications of occult societies point to this, speakers support it, and appliances are made and sold, which facilitate all this nonsense, and thus almost the entire occult world acts as *an efficient underling of the Darkness*, in the honest conviction of being a priest of the Light!

These occurrences alone prove the utter ignorance that lies in occult endeavours of this kind! They show that of all these people nobody is really a *"seeing"* one! If now and then some good medium has developed from these beginnings, or rather, to be more correct, if in the early stages a good medium has been temporarily attracted to them, this must not be regarded as proof to the contrary.

The few people destined for this from the outset have in their own natural development a totally different protection, carefully watching over every step, which others do *not* enjoy. However, this protection is only effective in natural self-development, *without any artificial aids!* Because only in all that is natural does protection lie as a matter of course.

As soon as there is the slightest assistance, whether through practices by the person concerned or from another source in the form of magnetic sleep or hypnotism, it becomes unnatural, and is thus no longer completely in harmony with the Natural Laws which can alone grant protection. When to this there is added ignorance such as exists everywhere today, then it becomes disastrous. *Volition* alone will never replace ability when it comes to action. But no one should go further than his own ability will carry him.

It is naturally possible that among the hundreds of thousands who engage in this dangerous pastime there may be here and there one who really escapes unpunished and enjoys good protection. There are also many who will only be harmed in such a way as is not yet apparent on earth; and not until they pass on must they suddenly realise in what follies they have actually indulged. But there are also many who already bear physical evidence of harm, although they will never recognise the real cause during their life on earth.

For this reason the ethereal and spiritual happenings during these pastimes must for once be explained. It is just as simple as everything in Creation, and not at all so complicated, and yet again more difficult than many imagine.

In the present state of the earth the *Darkness* has, through the volition of mankind, gained the upper hand over everything material. Thus in all material things it stands to all intents and purposes on its own familiar ground, and can therefore manifest to the fullest extent in the material. Hence it is in its element there, fighting on soil with which it is well acquainted. Thereby, for the time being, in all that is material, that is gross material, it is superior to the Light.

The consequence is that in all things material the power of the Darkness becomes greater than that of the Light. Now with such pastimes as table-turning, etc., the Light, thus what is exalted, is completely out of the question. At the most we can speak of something bad, thus dark, and something better, thus more luminous.

Now when a person makes use of a table, or a glass, or indeed of any gross material object, he thus enters upon the battle-ground which is familiar to the Darkness. A soil which all Darkness calls its own. From the start he thereby yields to the Darkness a power against which he cannot summon up adequate protection.

Let us for a moment consider a spiritist pastime, or simply a party game with the table, and then follow the spiritual, or rather the ethereal happenings.

When one or more persons approach a table for the purpose of contacting through it those living in the beyond, either so that these should make knocking sounds or, as is more usual, move the table, so that words can be formed from these signs, then through the connection with material substance the first to be attracted is also the Darkness, which will take over the manifestations.

Those in the beyond often use high-sounding language with great skill, and seek to answer the thoughts of men, which they can read quite easily, in the manner these desire; but if serious questions arise they invariably lead them astray and, if it is done often, try gradually to bring them under their ever-increasing influence, and so slowly but surely to drag them down. Yet they very cunningly leave the dupes in the belief that they are ascending.

But if perhaps at the very start, or at some other opportunity, a relative or friend who has passed over can communicate through the table, which very often happens, the deception is then much more easily accomplished. The people will recognise that it must really be a specific friend who manifests, and then will believe that it is always he when any utterances are transmitted through the table and the name of the friend is given as the author.

But this is not the case! Not only does the ever watchful Darkness make cunning use of the name to make deceptions appear as authentic as possible, and gain the confidence of the questioners; but it even goes so far that a dark one will interfere in the middle of a sentence begun by the real friend, and purposely give it a false ending. Thereupon emerges the scarcely known fact that in a smoothly and flowingly given sentence *two* have taken part. First the real, and perhaps quite luminous, therefore purer friend, and then a dark entity of evil volition, without the questioner noticing anything of it.

The results of this are easy to imagine. The trusting person is deceived and his faith shaken. The opponent uses the incident to support his ridicule and doubts, and occasionally to make violent attacks on the whole subject. But in fact both are wrong, which can only be traced back to the ignorance still prevailing on the whole matter.

What occurs, however, takes place in all naturalness: If a more luminous and real friend is at the table to comply with the wish of the questioner and to

96

make himself known, and a dark spirit crowds to the table, then the more luminous one must retreat from it, since the darker one can develop greater
strength through the material substance of the table acting as an intermediary,
because at the present time all that is material is the actual domain of the
Darkness.

The mistake is made by the person who chooses material objects, and thus
from the outset provides unequal ground. What is dense, heavy, and therefore dark, certainly stands by virtue of its density nearer to gross matter than
what is luminous, pure and lighter, and through the closer connection it can
develop greater strength.

On the other hand what is more luminous and still able to manifest through
a material object, likewise still possesses a certain degree of density corresponding with the object, otherwise a link with physical matter for the purpose of some communication would no longer be possible at all. This in itself
presupposes a closer approach to matter, which in turn involves the possibility of defilement as soon as the connection with the Darkness is made
through matter.

To avoid this danger the more luminous one has no option but quickly to
withdraw from the material, thus from the table or some other appliance, as
soon as a dark one reaches out for it, in order to cut off the intermediary link,
which would form a bridge over the natural separating and thereby protecting gulf.

It is then unavoidable in the beyond that in such cases the person experimenting through the table must be left at the mercy of base influences. Indeed, his own action proves that he wished for nothing else; *for ignorance of
the Laws cannot protect him here either.*

With these occurrences much that has hitherto been inexplicable will become clear to many, numerous puzzling contradictions will be solved, and it
is to be hoped that in future many people will really leave such dangerous
playthings alone!

Also the dangers attaching to all other experiments, which are much bigger
and more powerful, can now be described in the same detailed manner. But
for the time being it should suffice to mention these most common and wide-
spread instances.

Only one other danger must yet be mentioned. Through this kind of
questioning and seeking for replies and advice, people make themselves very

dependent and lose their self-reliance. This is the reverse of life's purpose on earth.

In every respect it is the wrong course! It only brings harm, no benefit. It is a grovelling on the ground where there is danger of constantly encountering disgusting vermin, wasting one's strength, and finally collapsing exhausted by the wayside ... all for nothing!

With this "desire to investigate", however, much damage is also done to those in the beyond!

Many dark ones are thus offered an opportunity, indeed they are thereby even directly tempted to commit evil and to burden themselves with fresh guilt, which they could not so easily do otherwise. And others are retarded in their upward striving through the constant link formed by such wishes and thoughts.

In clearly observing the nature of these investigations it often appears so childishly obstinate, so imbued with a most ruthless egotism, and withal so clumsy, that one must shake one's head and ask oneself how anyone could possibly want to open out to the general public a region of which he himself does not really know the first thing.

It is also wrong for all these investigations to take place before the general public. To do so opens the way for visionaries and charlatans, making it difficult for mankind to gain confidence.

This has never happened in any other field. And every investigation whose complete success is now acknowledged was subject to numerous failures during the previous period of research. But the public were not allowed to take part in them to the same extent! They are fatigued by them, and in due course lose all interest. The result is that when the Truth is at last discovered the impetus for a revolutionary and sweeping enthusiasm was bound to be lost beforehand. Mankind can no longer rouse themselves to an exultant joy, so convincing that it carries everything along with it.

When it is realised what wrong courses have been pursued, the repercussions become sharp weapons in the hands of many enemies, who in the course of time are able to instil such distrust in the minds of hundreds of thousands of people that, when the Truth emerges, these unfortunates will no longer desire to examine it seriously for sheer fear of a new delusion! They close their ears, which they would otherwise have opened, and so miss the last span of time that could still grant them the opportunity to ascend to the Light.

Thereby the Darkness will then have won a further victory! It can offer its gratitude to the investigators who to that end extended their hands to it, and who are pleased and proud to proclaim themselves leaders of modern psychic sciences!

WITH few exceptions, mankind labour under a boundless delusion which is fatal for them!

God has no need to run after them and beg them to believe in His existence. Nor are His servants sent out forever to admonish people on no account to turn away from Him. This would indeed be absurd. To think and expect such things is a dishonouring and debasing of the sublime Godhead.

This erroneous conception causes great harm. It is fostered by the behaviour of many truly earnest pastors who, out of a real love for God and men, try again and again to convert people who turn only to material things, to convince them and win them over to the church. All this only tends immeasurably to increase man's conceit in regard to his importance, of which there is more than enough already, and in the end really to place many under the delusion that they must be begged to strive for what is good.

This is also the cause of the strange attitude of the majority of all "believers", whose example is more often a deterrent than an inspiration. Thousands upon thousands feel a certain inner satisfaction, an exaltation, in the consciousness that they believe in God, that they utter their prayers with such earnestness as they are capable of bringing up, and that they do not intentionally harm their neighbours.

In this inner "exaltation" they feel a certain reward for goodness, thanks from God for their obedience, and they sense a being linked with God, of Whom they also think at times with a certain sacred thrill that produces or leaves behind a state of bliss, in which they revel.

But these legions of believers take the wrong course. Living happily in a self-created delusion, they are unaware that it numbers them with those Pharisees who, with the genuine but mistaken feeling of gratitude, bring their small sacrifices: "Lord, I thank Thee that I am not as other men are". This is not expressed in words, nor really in thought, but the inner "uplifting feeling" is nothing more than this unconscious prayer of thanks, which Christ too has already shown to be false.

In these cases the inner "exaltation" is nothing more than the setting free of self-satisfaction engendered by prayer or forced good thoughts. Those who call themselves humble are mostly very far from really being humble! It often requires self-restraint to speak with such believers. In such a frame of mind they will never at any time attain to the bliss which they are confident they already possess! Let them take heed lest they be altogether lost through their spiritual arrogance, which they consider to be humility.

It will be easier for many who now are still absolute unbelievers to enter the Kingdom of God than for all the legions with their conceited humility, who do not really stand before God in simple supplication, but indirectly demanding that He reward them for their prayers and pious words. Their petitions are demands, their inner being hypocritical. They will be swept away like empty chaff before His Countenance. They will have their reward, certainly, but it will be different from what they imagine. They have already satiated themselves long enough on earth in the consciousness of their own value.

The feeling of well-being will rapidly disappear on passing into the Ethereal World, where the inner intuitive perception, which is scarcely sensed here, will come to the fore, while the feeling hitherto mainly produced only by thoughts will be blown to nothing.

This inner, silent, so-called humble expectation of something better is really nothing but a demand, even though it be expressed differently, in however beautiful words.

Every demand, however, is a presumption. God alone has to demand! Nor did Christ come pleading to mankind with His Message, but warning and demanding. He certainly gave explanations about the Truth, but He did not enticingly hold out rewards before the eyes of His hearers to spur them on to become better. Calmly and sternly He commanded serious seekers: "Go thou and do likewise!"

God stands before humanity *demanding*, not enticing and pleading, not lamenting and grieving. He will calmly abandon to the Darkness all the wicked, even all the wavering ones, so that those who are striving upwards shall no longer be exposed to their attacks; enabling the others thoroughly to experience everything they consider to be right, and thus come to the recognition of their error!

LIKE deepest night ethereal darkness lies spread over this earth! For a very long time already. So dense and firm is the suffocating embrace in which it holds the earth that every ascending light-perception is like a flame which, without oxygen, loses its power and quickly fading dies out.

This ethereal condition, now manifesting at its worst, is dreadful. Anyone permitted for only five seconds to glimpse what is happening would from sheer horror be deprived of all hope of salvation! –

And all this has been brought about through the guilt of men themselves. Through the guilt of their propensity for what is base. Here mankind have been their own worst enemy. Now even those few who are once more earnestly striving upwards are *also* in danger of being swept into the depths, towards which others are now developing at a sinister speed.

It is like a close embrace, which is followed inevitably by fatal absorption. Absorption into the sultry, tenacious swamp, in which everything sinks without a sound. There is no longer a struggling, but only a still, silent, gruesome choking.

And man does not recognise it. Spiritual indolence blinds him to this fateful happening.

But all the time the swamp is sending forth its poisonous emanations, which slowly weary those who are still strong and alert, so that they, too, will fall asleep and sink away powerless.

That is the state of affairs on earth today. It is not a picture that I am unfolding therewith, but *life!* Since all ethereal matter bears forms, created and animated through men's intuitive perceptions, such a happening actually takes place continually. And this is the environment that awaits men when they must leave this earth, and cannot be led upwards to the more luminous and beautiful regions.

But the Darkness grows ever *more* dense.

Therefore the time draws near when for a while this earth must be left to the rule of Darkness, without direct help from the Light, because humanity enforced this through their volition. The consequences of the volition of the majority *were bound* to bring this ending. – It is the time which John was once permitted to behold, when God will veil His Countenance. –

Everywhere there is night. Yet during the deepest affliction when everything, including what is better, is also in danger of sinking away, at the same time dawn will now break! But the dawn will first bring the travail of a great purification, which is inevitable before the salvation of all serious seekers can begin; for *no* helping hand can be offered to all those who pursue base ends! They shall fall headlong into those terrible depths where alone they can still hope for an awakening through such torments that they must come to loathe themselves.

Those who with sneers and apparent impunity have hitherto been able to hinder the upward striving ones will become silent and more pensive, until finally, begging and whimpering, they will supplicate for the Truth.

Then it will not be so easy for such; they will be irresistibly led through the millstones of the inexorable Laws of Divine Justice, until in the *experiencing* they come to the recognition of their errors. –

In the course of my travels I could see that a firebrand was hurled among the indolent human spirits with my Word, which declares that no man can lay claim to Divinity; whereas just at this time much effort is bent upon discovering God *within* oneself, so that ultimately man himself might also become God!

Hence disquiet has often awakened with my Word, mankind rebelliously seeking to defend themselves against it, because they only wish to hear soothing and reassuring words that seem *pleasant* to them!

Those who so rebel are simply cowards, who would like nothing better than to evade the personal issue, only to remain in obscurity, where they can indulge in sweet and peaceful dreams to *their* heart's content.

Not everyone can bear to be exposed to the Light of Truth, which clearly and mercilessly shows up the defects and spots on one's garment.

With smiles, scoffing or with enmity such people would like to prevent the coming of the day when the feet of clay supporting that flimsily constructed idol, their "ego", will be clearly revealed. Such fools are only masquerading with themselves, which will be relentlessly followed by the grey Ash Wednesday. With their wrong views they really want only to idolise themselves, and thereby they feel well and comfortable on earth. From the outset they regard *anyone* who disturbs them from this indolent placidity as an enemy! However, *this time* no resistance will be of any avail to them!

The self-idolatry evident in the assertion that there is Divinity in man is a base attempt to grasp at the sublimity and purity of your God, *thereby defiling* for you the most Holy, to which you look up in the most blissful trust! –

There is within you an altar which should serve for the worship of your God. This altar is your intuitive faculty. If this is pure it is directly connected with the Spiritual Realm and thus with Paradise! Then there are moments when you too can fully perceive the nearness of your God, as often happens in times of deepest sorrow and greatest joy!

You then perceive His nearness in the same way as is constantly experienced by the eternal Primordial Spirits in Paradise, with whom you are closely connected at such moments. The strong vibration caused by the emotion of great joy or deep sorrow for a few seconds pushes everything earthly and low far into the background, thereby setting free the purity of the intuitive perception, which thus immediately forms the bridge to the homogeneous purity that animates Paradise!

This is the most supreme happiness for the human spirit. The eternal ones in Paradise live in it continually. It brings the glorious certainty of being protected. They are then fully conscious of the nearness of their great God, in Whose Power they stand, yet at the same time they also realise as a matter of course that they have reached their greatest height, and will never be able to behold God.

This, however, does not depress them, but in the recognition of His unapproachable Majesty they give jubilant thanks for the inexpressible mercy He has always shown in regard to the arrogant creature.

And this happiness can already be enjoyed by man on earth. It is quite right to say that in deeply solemn moments earthman senses the nearness of his God. But it is sacrilege if man asserts that he himself possesses a spark of the Godhead within, because of this wonderful bridge which grants him the awareness of Divine nearness.

Hand in hand with this assertion also goes the debasing of Divine Love. How can God's Love be measured by the standard of human love? Moreover, how can It be valued even *below* this human love? Look at those people who picture Divine Love as the highest ideal, just silently enduring and also forgiving everything! They want to recognise Divinity *by the fact* that It tolerates any misbehaviour from lower *creatures,* such as only the greatest weakling or the most cowardly human being would do, for which they are despised. Just reflect what a monstrous insult this implies!

Men would like to sin unpunished, and then finally even please their God by allowing Him to forgive their wrong-doing without having to atone for it themselves! Such presumption shows either the utmost narrow-mindedness, unpardonable laziness, or the realisation of how hopelessly weak they are in bringing forth the good volition to strive upwards: The one, however, is as reprehensible as the other.

Picture to yourselves Divine Love! Crystal clear, radiant, pure and great! Can you then imagine that It is as sentimentally weak and ignobly yielding as mankind would so like it to be? They want to build up a false greatness where they *wish* for weakness, they give a false picture only to deceive and reassure themselves about their own shortcomings, which make them willing servants of the Darkness.

Where then is to be found the freshness and power that unquestionably belong to the crystal purity of Divine Love? Divine Love is inseparable from the utmost severity of Divine Justice. Indeed It even is Divine Justice. Justice is Love, and Love again lies only in *Justice.* In this alone lies also Divine Forgiveness.

The churches are right in saying that God forgives *everything!* And *really* forgives! Contrary to man, who goes on condemning a person even after he has atoned for some trivial offence, and thus burdens himself with a double guilt by such thoughts, because he does not act according to the Will of God. Here human love is lacking in justice.

The activity of the Divine Creative Will purifies every human spirit of its guilt as soon as it strives upwards, whether through its own experiences or through its voluntary efforts at improvement.

If it returns to the Spiritual Realm from these mills in the World of Matter, it will then stand pure in the Kingdom of its Creator; it matters not *what* its guilt may have been! Just as pure as one who has never yet sinned. But *first* his path will take him through the activity of the Divine Laws, and in *this* fact lies the guarantee of Divine Forgiveness, of His Mercy!

Do we not often hear today the fearful questioning: How could God allow such years of tribulation? Where does love, where does justice come in? The question is asked by *mankind*, by *nations*, often by families and the individual human being! Should this not rather prove to him that, *after all*, God's Love is probably *different* from what many would like to imagine it? Just try *in this way* to visualise to the *end* the all-forgiving Love of God, as man insists on portraying It! Demanding no self-atonement, tolerating everything, and ultimately even offering generous forgiveness. It must produce a lamentable result! Does man consider himself so precious that his God should suffer under this? Thus more precious even than God Himself? To what lengths does men's presumption go. –

On thinking it over calmly you must stumble over a thousand obstacles, and can *only* come to a conclusion when you belittle God and make Him imperfect.

But He was, and is, and remains perfect, regardless of men's attitude to this.

His Forgiveness lies in *Justice*. Nothing else. And in this unconditional Justice also lies the great Love which has hitherto been so misunderstood!

Rid yourselves of the habit of measuring according to earthly standards! God's Justice and God's Love are concerned with the human *spirit*. Material substance has nothing whatever to do with this. It is only *formed* by the human spirit itself, and has no life without spirit.

Why do you so often torment yourselves with mere earthly trifles which you perceive to be sin, but which are not really so.

It is only what the *spirit wills* in any action that is decisive for the Divine Laws in Creation. This spiritual will, however, is not thought-activity, but the deepest intuitive perception, the actual volition within man, which alone can set in motion the Laws of the beyond, and indeed does so automatically.

Divine Love cannot be degraded by men; for in It rest in Creation also the inexorable Laws of His Will, Which is borne by Love. And these Laws take effect according to how man adjusts himself in Creation. They may link him with the proximity of his God, or they form a dividing wall that can never be destroyed unless man at last adapts himself to them, which means obeys them, in which alone he can find his salvation, his happiness.

It is *one* perfect whole, the great Work shows no flaws, no gaps. Any fool or simpleton who would have it otherwise will meet with his doom. –

Divine Love weaves therein only what *benefits* every human spirit, but not what pleases and seems agreeable to it on earth. Divine Love goes *far* beyond this, because it governs the whole of existence. –

At present many a person very often thinks: If tribulation and destruction are to be expected in order to bring about a great purification, then God must be so just as to send out in advance preachers calling for repentance. Man must certainly be forewarned. Where is John who proclaims what is to come?

These are wretched ones who think themselves so wise, but are so empty-minded! Such cries merely conceal an utterly hollow presumption. They would only scourge him and throw him into prison!

Do open your eyes and ears! But man goes *dancing* frivolously away over all the suffering and misery of his fellow-men! He does not *want* to see and hear! –

Already two thousand years ago a preacher also first appeared, calling for repentance, and following on his heels the Word Incarnate. Yet mankind have made strenuous efforts to efface and obscure the pure lustre of the Word, so that the magnetic power of Its radiance should gradually become extinct. –

And all those who wish to disentangle the Word from the clinging vines must soon perceive how desperately the messengers of Darkness try to prevent every joyful awakening!

But today there will be no recurrence of what happened in Christ's time! At that time the Word came! Mankind had their free will, and the majority then decided to reject and repudiate this Word! From that time onwards they were subject to the Laws, which were automatically linked to the free decision then carried out in this way. Thereafter men found all the fruits of their own volition on their self-chosen path.

Soon the ring will close. Things are piling up ever more, rising like a rampart which will soon collapse and crash down upon mankind, who go on living unsuspectingly in spiritual apathy. Finally, at the time of fulfilment, they will naturally no longer have the free choice!

They must now just reap what they sowed at that time, and also later on their wrong ways.

All who once rejected the Word at the time of Christ are today reincarnated on this earth to settle accounts. Now they no longer have the right to be forewarned, and to make a second decision. In the two thousand years they have had time enough to change their minds! Also he who absorbs a wrong interpretation of God and His Creation, and does not exert himself to grasp It more purely, has *not* absorbed It *at all*. Indeed, it is far worse, for a wrong belief keeps one back from grasping the Truth.

But woe unto him who, in order to attract followers, *falsifies* or *perverts* the Truth because men find it more agreeable in an easier form. He not only burdens himself with the guilt of falsification and deception, but in addition he also bears the whole responsibility for those whom he was able to attract to himself by making it more convenient or acceptable. When his hour of retribution comes he will *not* be helped. He will fall into the abyss from which there can be no return, and rightly so! – This John was also permitted to see and warn against in his Revelation.

And when the great purification begins man will now have no time to rebel, or even to stem this happening. The Divine Laws which man so much likes to picture wrongly will then take inexorable effect.

Just in the most terrible tribulation of the times that the earth has ever experienced, humanity will at last learn that God's Love is far removed from the softness and weakness which man so audaciously ascribed to It.

More than half of all the men living at the present time do not belong on this earth at all!

Already for thousands of years this mankind have sunk so low, and live *so* strongly in the Darkness, that through their unclean volition they have built many bridges to dark spheres which are far *below* this earth-plane. There live those who have sunk deeply, whose ethereal weight would never have permitted the possibility of their rising to this earth-plane.

This formed a *protection* both for all those living on earth and for these dark ones themselves. They are separated by the natural Law of Ethereal Gravity. Down below they can give full vent to their passions, and all baseness, without doing any harm. On the contrary. There their unrestrained indulgence only strikes those of a like nature, whose base way of living similarly also affects them. Thus they suffer mutually, which leads to maturing but not to further guilt. For through the suffering, loathing for themselves may in time awaken, and with it also the desire to escape from this region. Gradually the desire leads to an agonising despair, which may finally result in the most fervent prayers, and therewith in an earnest volition to do better.

This is how it should be. But through men's wrong volition things developed differently!

Through their *dark* volition men built a bridge to the region of Darkness. Thus they held out a hand to those living there, making it possible for them to rise to the earth through the power of attraction of similar species. Here they naturally also found the opportunity for a fresh incarnation, which was not yet intended for them in the normal course of world events.

For on the earth-plane, where through the medium of gross matter they can live *together* with those who are more luminous and better, they only do harm and thereby burden themselves with *fresh* guilt. This they cannot do in their lower regions; for the depravity is only beneficial to their homogeneous kind, because ultimately they only recognise themselves as they really are, and come to abhor their baseness, which helps towards improvement.

Man has now *disrupted* this normal course in all development through the base use of his free will, with which he formed ethereal bridges to the region of Darkness, so that those who had sunk there could be thrown onto the earth-plane like a rabble, who now joyfully populate the greater part of it.

Since luminous souls must retreat before the Darkness wherever the latter has gained a firm foothold, it was easy for the darker souls, who had no right to be on the earth-plane, also to incarnate sometimes where otherwise only a luminous soul would have entered. In such a case the dark soul has found an anchorage through some person near the prospective mother, enabling it to assert itself and push aside the light soul, even when mother or father belong to the more luminous ones.

This also clears up the puzzle of how many a black sheep could come to good parents. However, if a prospective mother takes more heed of herself and of her immediate surroundings, of those with whom she associates, this can *not* happen.

Thus one can recognise it only as *Love* when at last the final effect of the Laws sweeps away from the earth-plane in full justice those who do *not* belong here, so that they fall into that realm of Darkness to which by their nature they definitely belong. Thus they can no longer hinder the ascent of the more luminous ones, nor burden themselves with fresh guilt, but perhaps still, after all, mature through disgust at their own experiences. –

The time will certainly come when the hearts of *all* men will be seized with an iron grip, when spiritual arrogance will be uprooted in every human creature with terrible relentlessness. Then every doubt which today prevents the human spirit from recognising that Divinity is not *in* him, but high *above* him, will also disappear. That It can only stand as the purest *image* on the altar of his inner life, to which he looks up in humble prayer. –

It is no error but sin when a human spirit confesses his desire also to be Divine. Such presumption must cause his fall; for it is equivalent to an attempt to tear the sceptre from the Hand of his God, and degrade Him to the same level as man occupies, and on which until now he has never even fulfilled his task, because he wanted to be *more,* and aspires to heights which he can never possibly reach, nor even recognise. Thus he heedlessly overlooked all reality, not only making himself quite useless in Creation, but far worse, making himself directly *harmful!*

In the end, brought about through his own wrong attitude, it will be proved to him with uncanny clarity that in his present so degenerated state he does not even represent the shadow of Divinity. The whole hoard of earthly knowledge that he has laboriously accumulated over these thousands of years will then prove before the horrified gaze of his eyes to be as *nothing;* helpless, he will experience with himself how the fruits of his one-sided earthly aspirations become useless and sometimes even a curse to him. *Then he may reflect upon his own divinity, if he can! – –*

A mighty voice will sound forth and compel him: "Down on your knees, creature, before your God and Lord! Do not sacrilegiously try to lift yourself up to the level of God!" – –

The self-centredness of the indolent human spirit cannot continue.

Only then can this humanity really think of an ascent. That will also be the time when everything that does not stand on a sound foundation will collapse. The sham forms of life, the false prophets and the organisations surrounding them, will disintegrate from within! Therewith the wrong courses that have hitherto prevailed will also be exposed.

Then many a self-complacent person will probably also be terrified to realise that he is standing on the brink of an abyss and, through being wrongly guided, is swiftly gliding downwards when he proudly imagined himself already to be ascending and nearing the Light! That he opened protective gates without having the full strength of defence behind them. That he attracted dangers which in the natural course of events he would have passed over. Happy is he who then finds the right way back!

ONCE UPON A TIME...!

Four words only, yet they are like a magic formula; for they bear within them the quality of instantly arousing some special intuitive perception in every human being. Seldom is this intuitive perception of the same kind. Similar to the effect music has. Exactly as with music, these four words also find their way straight to the spirit of man, his real "ego". Naturally only to those who do not keep the spirit completely locked within them, and have thus already lost their real humanity here on earth.

On hearing these words, however, every *human being* will involuntarily and instantly think back to some former experience. This rises vividly before him, and with the picture also a corresponding intuitive perception.

With one it will be a yearning tenderness, a melancholy happiness, or also a silent longing impossible of fulfilment. With others, however, pride, anger, horror or hatred. Man will always think of some experience which made an exceptional impression upon him, but which he also thought long since extinguished within him.

Yet nothing has been extinguished in him, nothing lost of what he once really *experienced* within himself. All of it he can still call his own, as really acquired by himself, and thus imperishable. But only that which has been experienced! Nothing else can arise with these words.

Man should for once closely heed this with care and with an alert mind, then he will soon recognise what is really alive within him, and what can be designated as dead, as a soulless shell of useless memories.

Only what has so deeply affected him during his earth-life as to stamp an indelible and ineffaceable imprint on his *soul* serves to benefit man, by whom we must not imagine the physical body. Only such imprints have an influence on the forming of the human soul and thereby, going further, also on the advancement of the spirit for its continual development.

In reality, therefore, only *that* which leaves such a deep impression is experienced and thus made one's own. All else flits ineffectively by, or at best serves to help in the development of events that are capable of calling forth such great impressions.

Happy is he who can call his own many such powerful experiences, no matter whether called forth by joy or sorrow; for the impressions they leave will one day be the most precious that a human soul takes with it on its way into the beyond. –

Purely intellectual work, such as is customary today, *when properly applied* serves only to facilitate *physical* life on earth. Closely considered, that is the actual ultimate aim of *all* intellectual activity! In the final analysis there is never any other result. With *all* erudition, irrespective of which branch of education, and also with all activities whether in public affairs or in the family, with every individual or with nations, as also finally with humanity as a whole.

But unfortunately *everything* has subjected itself quite unconditionally to the intellect alone, and therefore lies in heavy chains of earthly limitation of the perceptive capacity, which was naturally bound to bring in its wake disastrous consequences in every activity and happening, and will continue to do so.

To this there is only *one* exception on this whole earth. This exception, however, is not perhaps offered to us by the church, as many will think and indeed as it should be, but by *art!* Here now the intellect unquestionably takes *second* place. But where the intellect gains the upper hand, art is at once reduced to *craftsmanship;* it is immediately and quite incontestably degraded from its lofty position. This is a logical consequence which in its simple naturalness cannot possibly be otherwise. Not one exception to it can be pointed out.

Of course, the same conclusion must also be drawn in all else! Does this not make man think? Surely it must be as though scales fell from his eyes. This quite plainly indicates to the thinking and discriminating person that with everything else dominated by the intellect he can indeed obtain but one substitute, the inferior! From this fact man should recognise the place assigned by nature to the intellect, if anything that is right and of value is to arise!

So far only art is still born out of the activity of the living spirit, out of the intuitive perception. Art alone has had a natural and therefore a normal and healthy origin and development. The spirit, however, does not *express* itself in the intellect, but in the *intuitive perceptions*, and only *manifests* in what is

112

generally called *"deep inner feeling" ("Gemuet")*. That is just what the intellectual man of today, who is so inordinately proud of himself, likes to mock and ridicule. Thus he derides what is most valuable in man, yes, the very thing that really makes man a human being!

Spirit has nothing to do with the intellect. If at length man wishes for improvement in all things he must take heed of Christ's words: *"By their works ye shall know them!"* The time is at hand when this will come to pass.

Only the works of the *spirit* from their very origin bear *life* within them, and with it permanence and stability. Everything else must collapse from within when its time of blossoming is past. As soon as the fruits of it are due to appear, the barrenness will be exposed!

Just look at history! Only the work of the spirit, that is to say art, has outlived the peoples who have already collapsed through the activity of their intellect, which in itself is lifeless and cold. Their great, much-praised knowledge could not offer them any salvation from collapse. Egyptians, Greeks and Romans went this way; later also the Spaniards and the French, now the Germans – *yet the works of genuine art have outlived them all!* Nor can they ever perish. But no one has perceived with what strict regularity these events have recurred. No person thought of getting to the real root of this great evil.

Instead of searching for this root, and for once calling a halt to the ever-recurring decline, men have blindly submitted to it, and with laments and complaints have resigned themselves to the idea that "nothing can be changed".

Now finally it will strike all mankind! Much misery already lies behind us, still greater is to come. And deep affliction moves through the dense ranks of those who have even now to some extent been affected by it.

Think of all the peoples who have already had to fall on reaching full bloom, the zenith of the intellect. The fruits which developed from the blossom-time were *everywhere the same!* Immorality, shamelessness and debauchery in various forms, inevitably followed by decline and ruin.

The complete similarity is very obvious to everyone! And also every thinking person must discover a very definite nature and consistency of the strictest Laws in this happening.

One after the other these peoples had finally to recognise that their greatness, their power and their glory were only apparent, upheld solely by force and compulsion, and not secured by an inner soundness.

If you would only open your eyes, instead of despairing! Look about you, learn from the past, and compare it with the messages that have reached you already thousands of years ago from the Divine, and you *must* discover the root of the devouring evil, which alone forms the obstacle to the ascent of all mankind.

Only when the evil has been thoroughly eradicated will the path to general ascent be open, not before. And this will then be lasting, because it will be animated by the living spirit, which has hitherto been impossible. –

Before going into this subject more deeply, I want to explain what spirit, as the only really living part in man, is. Spirit is not wit, and not intellect! Nor is spirit acquired knowledge. It is erroneous, therefore, to call a person "rich in spirit" because he has studied, read and observed much and knows how to converse well about it, or because his brilliance expresses itself through original ideas and intellectual wit.

Spirit is something entirely different. It is an independent *consistency*, coming from the world of its homogeneous species, which is different from the part to which the earth and thus the physical body belong. The spiritual world lies higher, it forms the upper and lightest part of Creation. Owing to its consistency, this spiritual part in man bears within it the task of returning to the Spiritual Realm, as soon as all the material coverings have been severed from it. The urge to do so is set free at a very definite degree of maturity, and then leads the spirit upwards to its homogeneous species, through whose power of attraction it is raised.*

Spirit has nothing to do with the earthly intellect, only with the quality which is described as "deep inner feeling" ("Gemuet"). To be rich in spirit, therefore, is the same as "having deep inner feelings" ("gemuetvoll"), but not the same as being highly intellectual.

Just to discover this difference more easily, man should now make use of the expression: "Once upon a time!" That alone will help very many seekers to find clarification. If they observe themselves carefully they can recognise what has so far proved beneficial to their *souls* in their earth-life, or what has merely served to ease the conditions of their life and work in the earthly environment. In other words, what is of value to them not only on earth but also in the beyond, and what serves only earthly purposes but remains valueless for the beyond. The one can be taken over by man, but the other he leaves

---

* Lecture: "I am the Resurrection and the Life...!"

behind on his departure as belonging only here, because it can be of no further use to him. What he leaves behind, however, is but the tool for earthly events, an aid for the *time on earth*, nothing more.

If a tool is not used solely as such, but is valued much more highly, it obviously cannot come up to the higher demands made upon it; it is in the wrong place and will thereby naturally also produce many kinds of deficiencies, which in time will have quite disastrous consequences.

The first and foremost of these tools is the *earthly intellect* which, as a product of the human brain, must bear within itself the limitation to which anything physical-gross-material by its own consistency is always subject. And the product cannot possibly be different from its origin. It always remains bound to the nature of the origin. Likewise the works that develop through the product.

For the intellect this naturally results in the most limited, purely earthly comprehensive capacity, closely bound to time and space. Since it originates in the World of Gross Matter, itself inert and with no life of its *own*, the intellect is also without living power. This condition, of course, is likewise perpetuated in all the activities of the intellect, for which it thereby remains impossible to impart life to its works.

In this inflexible natural happening lies the key to the unhappy events during man's life on this small earth.

We must at last learn to differentiate between the spirit and the intellect, the vital core of man and his tool! When this tool is placed *above* the living core, as it has hitherto been, the result will be something unsound, which even at its inception must bear within it the germ of death; and thereby the vital, the highest and most valuable part, is constricted, bound and cut off from its necessary activity, until in the inevitable collapse of the lifeless structure it rises free but incomplete from the ruins.

Instead of "once upon a time" let us now picture to ourselves the question: "What was it like in former times?" How different is the effect. The great difference is immediately perceived. The first question speaks to the intuitive perception, which is linked with the spirit. But the second question is directed to the intellect, and entirely different pictures emerge. From the outset they are limited, cold, without warmth of life, because the intellect has nothing else to give.

From the very beginning, however, mankind's greatest guilt has lain in placing this intellect, which can only produce what is incomplete and without life, on a high pedestal, and virtually dancing around it in worship. It was given a place that should have been reserved *for the spirit alone.*

This action is entirely opposed to the ordinances of the Creator and thus to nature, because these are anchored in what takes place in nature. Therefore nothing can lead to a true goal either, but everything must fail at the point where the harvest is due to set in. It cannot be otherwise, but is a natural happening that is to be expected.

Only in *purely technical science,* in all industry, is it different. This has reached great heights through the intellect, and will even advance much further in the future! This fact, however, serves to prove the truth of my explanations. Technical science in *all* its aspects is and will always remain purely earthly, lifeless. Now since the intellect likewise belongs to all that is earthly, it is able to develop brilliantly in the technical sciences, and can accomplish really great things. Here it stands in its right place, in its real task!

But wherever anything "living", thus purely *human,* has to be considered as well, the intellect by its nature is not adequate, and *must* therefore fail if it is not then guided by the spirit! For spirit alone is life. Success of a specific kind can always be achieved only by the activity of the homogeneous kind. The earthly intellect will therefore never be able to do spiritual work! For this reason placing the intellect above life has become the grave offence of this mankind.

Contrary to the creative, thus wholly natural ordinance, man has therewith directly *reversed* his task, and has, so to speak, turned it upside down by yielding the supreme place that belongs to the living spirit to the intellect, which comes in the second and purely earthly place. Through this it is again quite natural for man now to be obliged painfully to seek from below upwards, whereby the superimposed intellect, with its limited capacity to comprehend, obstructs any broader view, instead of his being able to look down from above through the spirit.

If he wishes to awaken he is compelled first to "transpose the lights". To put the intellect, which is now above, in the place given to it by nature, and restore the spirit to the supreme position. This necessary transposition is no longer so easy for the man of today. –

The change of order that men introduced in bygone times, so incisively directed against the Will of the Creator, thus against the Laws of Nature, was the actual *"fall of man"*, the consequences of which cannot be more terrible; for in due course it developed into "inherited sin", because the elevation of the intellect to the position of sole ruler again brought in its wake the natural consequence that, in the course of time, such one-sided cultivation and activity also strengthened the brain one-sidedly, so that only the part which has to do the work of the intellect grew bigger, and the other part was bound to become stunted. Thereby the part that has become stunted through neglect can only operate today as an unreliable dream-brain, even then being still under the powerful influence of the so-called day-brain, which activates the intellect.

Thus the part of the brain which should form the bridge to the spirit, or rather the bridge from the spirit to everything earthly, is thereby paralysed; a connection is broken, or at least very much loosened, whereby man has cut off for himself all spiritual activity, and with it also the possibility of "animating", spiritualising and inspiring his intellect.

Both parts of the brain should have been developed absolutely *equally,* for joint harmonious activity, like everything in the body. The spirit leading and the intellect carrying out here on earth. It is obvious that because of this all the activity of the body too, and even the body itself, can never be what it should be. For naturally what has taken place affects everything! Because the most essential factor for all earthly things is thereby missing!

It is easy to understand that the cutting off was simultaneously linked with the withdrawal and estrangement from the Divine. Indeed, there was no longer any way to It.

Finally this in turn had the disadvantage that already for thousands of years, owing to the ever-increasing hereditary factor, every child's body that is born brings with it to the earth the frontal intellectual brain so large that, from the outset and because of this condition, each child is again readily submitted to the intellect the moment this brain develops its full activity. The gulf beween the two parts of the brain has now grown so wide, and their functions so proportionately unequal, that with the majority of all mankind an improvement can no longer be achieved without catastrophe.

The intellectual man of today is no longer a *normal* human being, but lacks any development of the principal part of his brain that belongs to the complete human being, because he has allowed it to become stunted for thousands of years. Without exception, every intellectual has only a *crippled* normal brain! Therefore *brain-cripples* have been ruling the earth for thousands of years; they regard the normal human being as an enemy and seek to subjugate him. In their crippled condition they imagine that they accomplish a great deal, and they do not know that the normal human being is in a position to achieve *ten times as much,* producing works of a *permanent* nature which are more perfect than the present efforts! The way is open to every really serious seeker to acquire this ability!

An intellectual, however, will no longer so easily become able to grasp something that belongs to the activity of this stunted part of his brain! He is simply *incapable* of it, even if he should desire it; and solely because of his voluntary restriction he ridicules everything that he is unable to attain, and which owing to his really *retarded,* not normal brain will never at any time be understood by him either.

Just therein lies the most terrible part of the curse of this unnatural aberration. The harmonious co-operation of both parts of the human brain that absolutely belongs to a normal human being, is definitely impossible for the present-day intellectuals, who are called materialists. –

To be a materialist is really no recommendation, but evidence of a stunted brain.

Thus the *unnatural* brain has hitherto ruled on this earth; and finally its activity must obviously also bring about the inevitable collapse in all things, since everything, no matter what it wishes to produce, naturally contains discord and ill-health even from the very start, owing to the stunting.

Nothing of this can now be changed any more, but one must calmly let the naturally developing collapse come about. *Then, however, will be the day of resurrection for the spirit, and also for a new life!* The slave of the intellect, who has held the reins for thousands of years, will thus be disposed of for ever! Never again will he be able to arise, because the evidence and his own experience will finally compel him voluntarily to submit at last, ill and spiritually impoverished, to *that* which he was unable to grasp. Never again will he be given the opportunity to oppose the spirit, either by scoffing or by the semblance of right through imposing force, such as was also used towards the Son of God, Who had to fight against it.

Then there would still have been time to avert such misery. But now it is too late; for in the meantime the loosened connection between the two parts of the brain can no longer be bridged.

Many intellectuals will again try to ridicule the explanations in this lecture, but except for empty platitudes, they will be unable to present even *one really objective counter-argument*. Yet any serious seeker and thinker will have to take such blind zeal simply as fresh proof of what I have set forth herein. However hard they try, it is *impossible* for these people. Let us therefore regard them from now on as sick persons, who will soon be in need of help, and ... let us calmly await the time.

No struggle and no act of violence are needed to enforce the necessary progress; for the end will come of itself. Here too, through the immutable Laws of all reciprocal actions, the natural course of events will take effect quite inexorably, and also punctually. – –

Then, according to various prophecies, a "new generation" shall arise. However, this will not only be made up of the newly-born, such as are now already observed in California and also in Australia to be endowed with a "new sense", but mainly of *people already living,* who in the near future will become "seeing" through the many impending events. They will then possess the same "sense" as those now newly-born; for this is nothing more than the ability to stand in the world with an open and unrestrained spirit, no longer allowing itself to be suppressed by the limitation of the intellect. *Inherited sin will thereby be eliminated!*

But all this has nothing to do with what has been hitherto described as "occult faculties". *It is then simply the normal man as he should be!* To "become seeing" has nothing to do with "clairvoyance", but signifies *"insight"*, recognition.

Men will then be in the position to observe everything impartially, which means nothing else than to assess. They will see the intellectual man as he really is, with the limitation so dangerous to himself and his environment, in which there simultaneously arise the arrogant lust for power, and the disputing that is actually part of it.

They will also see how, with strict consistency, all humanity has suffered under this yoke in one form or another for thousands of years; and how this cancerous sore, as the hereditary enemy, has always been directed against the development of the free human *spirit,* which is the main object in human existence! Nothing will escape them, also not the bitter certainty that affliction, *all* suffering, and every downfall, were bound to come about through this evil, and that there could never be any betterment because

119

from the start all insight was ruled out owing to the limitation of the perceptive capacity.

But with *this* awakening all influence, all power of these intellectuals has ceased. For *all* time; for then begins a new and better epoch for mankind, in which the old can no longer survive.

Therewith the necessary victory of the spirit over the failing intellect, already longed for by hundreds of thousands today, will come. Many of the masses who have hitherto been led astray will then still recognise that until now they had completely misinterpreted the term "intellect". The majority simply accepted it as an idol, without examination, just because the others also did so; and because all its adherents always knew how through force and the laws to pose as infallible, absolute rulers. That is why many do not even take the trouble to expose the real hollowness of these people, and the deficiencies it has concealed.

There are certainly also some who already for decades have been fighting against this enemy with tenacious energy and conviction, in secret and to some extent also openly, occasionally also being exposed to most bitter suffering. *But they fight without knowing the real enemy!* And this has naturally made success more difficult. Indeed, it has made it impossible from the outset. The warriors' sword was not well sharpened, because they were always striking at non-essential things that dented it. With these non-essentials, however, they have always struck to one side, missing the mark, wasting their own strength, and only causing disunion among themselves.

In reality there is only *one* enemy of mankind all along the line: *The hitherto unrestricted rule of the intellect! That* was the great *fall of man,* his most grievous guilt, which brought all evil in its wake. *That* became the *hereditary sin,* and *that also is the Antichrist* of whom it is proclaimed that he will raise his head. More plainly expressed: The mastery of the intellect is his tool, through which men have fallen prey to him. To him, the enemy of God, the Antichrist himself ... Lucifer!*

We are in the midst of this time! He dwells today in *every* human being, ready to ruin him; for his activity immediately brings estrangement from God as quite a natural consequence. As soon as he is allowed to rule he cuts off the spirit.

* Lecture: "The Antichrist"

Therefore, let man be keenly on his guard. –

He must not on that account belittle his intellect, but must make it what it is, *his tool;* not, however, his authoritative will. Not his master!

The man of the coming generation will be able to regard past times only with disgust, horror and shame. Rather as we feel on entering an old torture chamber. There, too, we perceive the evil fruits of the cold, calculating domination of the intellect. For it is surely quite undeniable that a person *possessing only a little inner feeling,* and thus spiritual activity, could never have devised such atrocities! Still, on the whole it is no different today, only somewhat more camouflaged; and the miseries of the masses are just as rotten fruits as was the individual torture in olden times.

On looking back into the past, man will only be able to shake his head in sheer amazement. He will ask himself how it was possible to suffer these errors calmly for thousands of years. The answer, of course, is simple: by force! Wherever one looks it can be recognised quite clearly. Leaving aside the times of remote antiquity, we need only enter the aforementioned torture chambers which can still be seen everywhere today, and the use of which does not lie so very far back.

We shudder as we look at these old implements. What cold brutality, what bestiality do they reveal! Hardly anyone today will doubt that the most grievous crime lay in those past proceedings. Upon the criminals an even greater crime was thus perpetrated. But also many an innocent person, dragged away from family and freedom, was roughly cast into these dungeons. What lamentations, what shrieks of suffering died away here from those who, completely defenceless, were at the mercy of their tormentors. People were compelled to suffer things the contemplation of which simply fills one with horror and loathing.

Involuntarily every one asks himself whether it was really humanly possible – all that happened to these defenceless ones, and moreover under the guise of justice. Of a justice that after all once had only been obtained by force. And now again, through physical pain, confessions of guilt were forced from those under suspicion, so that they could then be murdered at leisure. Even though these confessions of guilt were only extracted under compulsion, in order to escape these insane physical tortures, yet they nevertheless satisfied the judges, because they needed them to comply with the ''letter'' of the law. Did these so narrow-minded ones really imagine that in this way they could also whitewash themselves before the Divine Will, and escape the inexorable working of the basic Law of Reciprocal Action?

Either all those who dared to pass judgment on others were the scum of the most hardened criminals, or it clearly showed the unhealthy limitation of the earthly intellect. There can be nothing between.

According to the Divine Laws of Creation every person in authority, every judge, no matter what office he holds here on earth, should never stand in his *actions* under some protection of his office, but like any other person he must alone and purely *personally, unprotected,* bear full responsibility *himself* for all he does in his office. Not only in the spiritual but also in the earthly sense. Then everyone would regard things much more seriously and carefully. And so-called "errors", whose consequences are forever irreparable, will certainly not so easily occur again. To say nothing of the physical and psychic suffering of the victims and their relatives.

But let us further consider another aspect of this subject, the trials of so-called "witches"!

Anyone who has ever had access to the court records of such trials would wish, in an outburst of burning shame, never to be numbered among this mankind. In those days if anyone even had knowledge of healing herbs, either through practical experience or tradition, and if he used this knowledge to aid sufferers asking him for help, he was relentlessly tortured for it. Final release from these tortures only came with death at the stake, if his body had not already succumbed to these cruelties.

Even physical beauty, especially chastity that did not yield willingly, could in those days give rise to such tortures.

And then the horrors of the Inquisition! Comparatively speaking, only a few years separate us from "that time"!

Just as today we recognise this injustice, so also did the populace feel at that time. For the "intellect" had not yet limited them to such an extent, and here and there the intuitive perception, the spirit, broke through in them.

Do we not recognise today the absolute narrow-mindedness in all this? The irresponsible stupidity?

Although these things are spoken of with an air of superiority and a shrugging of the shoulders, yet fundamentally nothing has changed. The stupid presumption towards everything not understood is still exactly the same! Except that instead of these tortures men now publicly scoff at everything which, owing to their narrow-mindedness, they do not understand.

Many a person would do better to search his heart for once and think seriously about this without sparing himself. Upholders of the intellect, which means those who are not quite normal, and often even the law courts, will from the outset regard as a swindler every person who possesses the ability to know something that is concealed from others; he may be able also to see the Ethereal World with his ethereal eyes as a natural occurrence, which will very soon no longer be doubted, much less brutally opposed.

And woe unto him who does not himself know what to make of it, but naively speaks of what he has seen and heard. He must fear the consequences as did the first Christians under Nero, with his helpers always ready for murder.

Should he even possess still other abilities which can *never* be grasped by the out-and-out intellectuals, then he will most certainly be mercilessly hunted, slandered and ostracised unless he complies with everyone's wishes; if at all possible he will be rendered "harmless", as it is so charmingly expressed. Nobody has any qualms of conscience about it. Even today such a man is regarded as the free prey of anyone, and sometimes of inwardly very unclean persons. The more narrow-minded, the greater the delusion of cleverness and the propensity to conceit.

Man has learned nothing from these happenings of the olden days, with their tortures, burnings at the stake, and records of ridiculous trials! For even today anyone is still free to defile and insult with impunity all that is unusual and not understood. In this respect it is no different now from what it was then.

The proceedings of the Inquisition, which were instigated by the Church, were even worse than those of the courts of law. Here the shrieks of the tortured were drowned by pious prayers. It was a mockery of the Divine Will in Creation! The ecclesiastical representatives of those days thus proved that they had no idea of Christ's true teaching, nor of the Godhead and Its Creative Will, Whose Laws lie irrevocably anchored and work on in Creation, the same even from the very beginning to the end of time.

God endowed the human spirit by its very nature with the free will to decide. Only through *this* can it mature *as it should*, refine itself and develop fully. Only therein lies the possibility for it to do so. However, should this free will be cut off, then this is a hindrance, if not a violent throwing back.

But in those days the Christian churches, as well as many religions, fought this Divine ordinance, opposing it with the greatest cruelty. By means of torture and finally death, they sought to compel people to pursue courses and make confessions which were against their conviction, thus *against their will*. Thereby they violated the Divine commandment. And not only that, but they hindered men's spiritual progress, even throwing them back centuries.

If only a spark of real intuitive perception, thus of the spirit, had shown itself, this should and could never have happened! Therefore such barbarities were only the cold-blooded work of the intellect.

As history proves, many a Pope even permitted the use of poison and dagger to realise his purely earthly wishes and aims. *That* could only happen under the domination of the intellect, which in its triumphal march subjugated *everything* and stopped at nothing. –

And supreme over all the Will of our Creator inexorably manifested and manifests in the irrevocable march of events. On passing into the beyond every human being is divested of earthly power and its protection. Name, position, everything is left behind. Only a poor human soul passes over, there to receive and experience what it sowed. Not a *single* exception is possible! On its path it is led through all the wheels of the relentless reciprocal action of Divine Justice. There is no church, no state, but only individual human souls who must personally account for every error they have made!

He who acts against God's Will, and thus commits a sin in Creation, is subject to the consequences of this transgression. It matters not who he may be and on what pretext he acted. Be it an individual under the cloak of the church or of the law ... a crime committed against body or soul is and remains a crime! Nothing can alter it, not even the *semblance* of justice, which is by no means always justice; for of course the laws, too, were made only by intellectuals, and therefore must be subject to earthly limitations.

Just consider the law in so many states, especially in Central and South America. The man who today presides over the government, enjoying all the honours connected with it, may even tomorrow be thrown into prison or executed as a criminal, if his opponent succeeds in seizing the reins of this government through an act of violence. Should he not be successful, then it is *he* who, instead of being recognised as the ruler, will be looked upon as a criminal and persecuted. And all the public officials are as willing to serve the one as the other. Even a world traveller, to remain in good standing everywhere, must change his conscience as often as he would his clothes when passing from one country to another. What in one country is considered a crime is very often permitted in another and, what is more, may even be welcomed.

This is naturally only possible in the achievements of the earthly intellect, but never where the intellect must occupy its natural place as a tool of the living spirit; for he who listens to the spirit will never neglect the Laws of God. And where these are used as the foundation there can be no flaws, no gaps, but only a uniformity that brings in its wake happiness and peace. In their basic features the expressions of the spirit can always and only be exactly the same everywhere. They will never contradict each other.

Also the arts of justice, healing and statesmanship are bound to remain merely deficient crafts where only intellect can form the foundation, and the spiritual is lacking in them. It cannot possibly be otherwise. Here naturally always starting from the true conception of "spirit". –

Knowledge is a product, but spirit is life, the value and power of which can only be measured according to its connection with the origin of the spiritual. The closer this connection the more valuable and powerful will be the part which emanated from the origin. But the looser this connection becomes, the more distant, alien, isolated and weak must also be the emanated part, thus the human being concerned.

All these are such simple self-evident facts that it is impossible to comprehend how the erring intellectuals can pass them by over and over again as if they were blind. For what the root provides, sustains the trunk, the blossom and the fruit! But here also this hopeless self-limitation in understanding reveals itself. They have toiled to erect a wall before themselves which they can now no longer see over, much less see through.

However, with their conceited, superior and mocking smile, with their arrogance and looking down upon others less deeply enslaved, they must sometimes appear to all spiritually alive people like poor, sick fools who, in spite of all pity, must be left to their delusion, because their limited understanding even allows facts that prove the contrary to slip by without making any impressions. Every effort to bring about an improvement must simply prove as fruitless as trying to heal a sick person by hanging a new and resplendent cloak around his shoulders.

Even today materialism is past its climax, and now, failing everywhere, it must soon collapse. Not without also tearing down much that is good. Its devotees are already at the end of their ability, and will soon become confused about their work and then about themselves, without perceiving the abyss that has opened up before them. They will soon be like a flock without shepherds, one not trusting the other, each pursuing his own way, and yet still proudly looking down upon others. Not thinking matters out carefully, but merely following old habits.

With all signs of the outward semblance of their hollowness, they will end by blindly falling into the abyss. They still regard as spirit what are only the products of their own brains. But how can lifeless matter produce living spirit? They are proud of their meticulous thinking in many things, but quite unscrupulously and most irresponsibly leave gaps in the most important.

Every new step, every attempt at improvement, will ever again have to carry within it all the barrenness of the intellectual work, and thus the germ of inevitable doom.

All that I am saying here is neither prophecy nor loose prediction, but the unalterable consequence of the all-animating Creative Will, Whose Laws I explain in my lectures. He who follows with me in spirit along the paths that are clearly indicated therein must also survey and recognise the necessary end. And all the signs for it are already here.

People complain and cry out, they see with disgust how the excrescences of materialism today take on scarcely believable forms. They beg and pray for deliverance from the affliction, for improvement and recovery from the overwhelming downfall. The few who have managed to save some stirring of their inner life from the tidal wave of the incredible happenings, who have not suffocated spiritually in the general downfall that deceptively bears the name of "progress" proudly on its brow, feel like outcasts and backward people, and are also regarded and ridiculed as such by the soulless followers of modern life.

A laurel wreath to all those who had the courage to refrain from joining the masses! Who have proudly stayed behind on the steeply sloping path!

He who today still considers himself unfortunate because of this must be a *sleepwalker! Open your eyes!* Do you not see that everything that oppresses you is already the beginning of the sudden end of materialism, which at the moment only appears still to rule? The whole structure is already collapsing, without any assistance from those who have suffered and must still suffer under it. Intellectual mankind must now reap what for thousands of years they have produced, nourished, reared and acclaimed.

In human reckoning it is a long time, but for God's self-acting mills in Creation a brief span. Wherever you look there is failure everywhere. It surges back and heaps itself up menacingly like a heavy rampart that will soon topple over and crash down upon its admirers, burying them beneath the ruins. It is the inexorable Law of Reciprocal Action which during this manifestation must have a terrible effect, because in spite of the many kinds of experiences gained there has never in thousands of years been any change towards higher things, but on the contrary the same wrong road has been trampled wider and wider.

Despondent ones, the time is at hand! Hold up your heads, which you have so often had to hang in shame when injustice and stupidity were able to cause you such deep suffering. Now look calmly at the opponent today who thus sought to suppress you!

Already the fine raiment worn up till now is very badly tattered. The figure in its true form is at last visible through all the rents. The exhausted product of the human brain, the intellect, which allowed itself to be enthroned as spirit, less confident but no less conceited, looks forth confounded!

Just confidently take the bandage from your eyes and look about you more keenly. Alone the perusal of newspapers which are otherwise quite good reveals all sorts of things to the clearsighted. There are desperate efforts still to cling to all the old illusions. With arrogance, and often very coarse jokes, people seek to cover up the lack of comprehension that becomes more and more evident. A person will frequently use absurd language to judge something, of which in reality he has quite obviously no shred of understanding.

Today even people with quite good abilities helplessly take refuge in questionable courses rather than confess that so many things are beyond the grasp of their own intellect, on which alone they have hitherto sought to rely. They do not sense the absurdity of their behaviour, do not see the weaknesses which they only help to increase thereby. Confused and dazzled, they will soon stand face to face with the Truth, and mournfully look back over their bankrupt life, at last recognising with shame that stupidity lay just where they thought themselves wise.

What have things already come to today? *The man of muscle is the hero!*

Has an earnest scientist, who after decades of arduous research has discovered a serum giving protection and also help against fatal diseases year after year to hundreds of thousands, young and old, ever been able to celebrate such triumphs as a boxer, who with purely physical, crude brutality overpowers his fellow-man? Yet does this in any way benefit even one human *soul?* It is only earthly, all earthly, which means *low* in the whole Work of Creation! Entirely corresponding to the golden calf of intellectual activity. As the triumph of this so earthbound clay effigy of a monarch over narrow-minded mankind! – –

And no one sees this mad rush downwards into the gruesome abyss!

He who intuitively perceives this will still keep silent for the present, in the shameful awareness of being ridiculed in any case should he speak. It is already a wild frenzy in which, however, there is a dawning recognition of powerlessness. And with the growing awareness of *that* recognition people become even more rebellious, out of sheer obstinacy, out of vanity, and last but not least from fear and horror of the impending events. They simply *refuse* already to think of the end of this colossal error! Convulsively they cling to the proud structure built up over past millennia, which closely resembles the Tower of Babel, and which will end in the same way!

This hitherto uncurbed materialism carries within it a foreboding of death, which becomes more evident every month! –

Yet in many human souls, in all places, on the entire earth, something is astir! The radiance of the Truth is still only covered by a thin layer of old, false conceptions, which the first gust of a purification will sweep away, thus setting free the core, whose light will unite with that of so many others to unfold its cone of rays, rising like a fire of gratitude to the Realm of Pure Joy, to the Feet of the Creator.

That will be the time of the much-longed-for Millennium, which lies before us in brilliant promise as the great Star of Hope!

And with this the grievous *sin* of all mankind *against the spirit,* which has kept the spirit bound on earth through the intellect, is at last redeemed! Only *that* then is the right way back to what is natural, to the way of the Will of the Creator, Who desires men's works to be great, and suffused with living intuitive perceptions! The victory of the spirit, however, will at the same time also be the victory of purest Love!

ERRORS

THERE is many a man who lifts up his eyes seekingly for Light and Truth. His longing is great, but very often he lacks earnest volition! More than half of the seekers are not genuine. They bring their own preconceived opinion. Should they have to change it in the slightest degree, then they would much rather reject all that is new to them, even if it contains the Truth.

Thus thousands must go under because, entangled as they are in erroneous convictions, they have restricted the freedom of movement which they need to swing themselves upward to salvation.

There are always some who imagine they have already grasped all that is right. They have no intention of subjecting *themselves* to a strict examination based on what they have heard and read.

I am naturally *not* addressing such as these!

Nor do I speak to churches and political parties, to fraternities, sects and societies, but only in all simplicity to *man* himself. Far be it from me to pull down what exists; for I am building up and completing the answers to questions as yet unsolved, questions that must arise in everyone as soon as he thinks just a little.

Only one basic condition is essential for every listener: Earnest seeking for the Truth. He should inwardly examine *the words* and let them come to life, but not heed the speaker. Otherwise he derives no benefit. All who do *not* strive to do this are simply wasting their time from the start.

It is incredible how naively the great majority of people cling tenaciously to their ignorance on such questions as whence they come, what they are, and whither they go!

Birth and death, the inseparable poles of all life on earth, should not be a secret to man.

There is a great deal of contradiction in the views of what constitutes the inner core of man. This is the result of the morbid self-aggrandisement of the earth-dwellers, who presumptuously boast that their inner core is *Divine!*

129

Look at humanity! Can you discover anything Divine in them? Such a foolish statement should be branded as blasphemy, because it denotes a debasement of Divinity.

Man does not carry a grain of Divinity within him!

This idea is just morbid presumption, the cause of which is simply the consciousness of being unable to understand. Where is the man who can honestly say that for him such a belief has also become conviction? Whoever examines himself seriously must deny it. He will feel distinctly that it is only a longing and a desire to harbour something Divine within him, but not a certainty! It is quite right to say that man carries within him a spark of God. But this *spark* of God is *spirit!* It is not a part of Divinity.

The term spark is a perfectly correct designation. A spark develops and flies out without taking along or bearing within it anything of the quality of the producer. It is the same here. A *spark* of God is not itself Divine.

Where such mistakes can already be found in regard to the *origin* of a being, there failure *must* ensue in the whole development! If I have built on a wrong foundation, then one day the whole structure must totter and fall.

For it is the origin that provides the *mainstay* for everyone's whole existence and development! Anyone who seeks to reach far beyond his origin, as usually happens, reaches for something he cannot grasp, and thereby loses all support in the quite natural course of events.

If, for instance, I reach for the branch of a tree which through its material consistency is similar to my earthly body, I can gain a hold on this branch and thus swing myself up on it.

But if I reach beyond this branch, then through the different consistency of the air I can find no support, and ... cannot therefore pull myself up either! Surely this is clear enough.

It is exactly the same with the *inner* consistency of man, called the soul, and its core, the spirit.

If this spirit wishes to have the essential support that it needs from its origin, then it must not of course seek to reach into the Divine. That would be unnatural; for the Divine lies much too far above it, and is of an entirely different consistency!

And yet in his conceit man seeks contact with that sphere to which he can never attain, and thus interrupts the natural order of things. His wrong desire is like a *dam* forming an obstruction between himself and his necessary supply of power from the origin. He cuts himself off from it.

Therefore away with such errors! Not until then can the human spirit develop its full power, which it still heedlessly disregards today, and become what it can and should be, *lord in Creation!* But mark well, only in Creation, not standing *above* it.

Only *Divinity* stands above all Creation! –

God Himself, the Origin of all being and life, is Divine, as the very word implies! Man was created by *His Spirit!*

Spirit is the *Will* of God. Now out of this *Will* the *first* Creation came into being. Do let us keep to this simple fact; it provides the possibility for a better understanding.

By way of comparison, just picture your own will. It is an act, but not part of man himself; otherwise man would in time dissolve in his many acts of will. There would be nothing whatever left of him.

It is no different with God! His Will created Paradise! But His Will is the Spirit, designated as the "Holy Spirit". Paradise, again, was only the *work* of the Spirit, not part of the Spirit Itself. There is a gradation *downwards* in this. The Creative Holy Spirit, that is, the Living Will of God, was not absorbed in His Creation. He did not even give one part of Himself to it; but He Himself remained wholly *outside* Creation. The Bible already states this quite clearly and plainly with the words: "And the *Spirit* of God moved *upon* the face of the waters", not God Himself! After all, that is different. Thus man does not carry within him anything of the Holy Spirit Itself either, but only of the *spirit* which is a work of the Holy Spirit, an act.

Instead of concerning himself with this fact, man already exerts all his energy to form a gap here! You have only to think of the prevalent conception of the *First* Creation, of Paradise! It absolutely had to be on this earth. The small human intellect thereby compressed the event requiring millions of years within its own sphere, limited by space and time, imagining himself to be the centre and axis of all that happens in the world. As a result he immediately lost the way to the actual starting-point of life.

In place of this clear path of which he could no longer command a view, a substitute had to be found in his religious conceptions, if he was not to designate himself as the creator of all being and life, and thus *as God*. The term "faith" has given him this substitute until now! And all mankind has

131

suffered ever since from the word "faith"! What is more, this misunderstood word, which was meant to restore all that was lost, became a cliff against which everything was wrecked!

Only the *indolent one* is content with faith. It is also faith which can become the butt of *scoffers*. And the word "faith", *wrongly* interpreted, is the barrier which today obstructs the road to mankind's progress.

Faith is not meant to be the cloak generously covering all slothful thinking, which like a sleeping-sickness gradually steals over and paralyses the spirit of man! Faith should really become *conviction*. Conviction however demands life, the keenest examination!

Where even *one* gap, *one* unsolved riddle remains, conviction becomes impossible. Therefore no one can have genuine faith so long as he has a question unanswered.

Even the words "blind faith" show that there is something unsound!

Faith must be *alive*, as Christ already once demanded, otherwise it serves no purpose. But to be alive means to bestir oneself, to weigh and also to examine! Not dumbly accepting the thoughts of others. After all, blind faith plainly means lack of understanding. What a person does not understand, however, cannot bring him spiritual benefit either, for through lack of understanding it cannot come to life within him.

But whatever he does not fully experience within never becomes his own either! And only what is his own helps him to ascend.

After all, no one can walk and go forward along a road containing great yawning clefts. Where man's knowledge cannot take him any further he must come to a spiritual standstill. This fact is irrefutable and no doubt also easily understood. Hence he who wishes to advance spiritually should awaken!

He can never proceed on his path to the Light of Truth in his sleep! Nor with a bandage or a veil over his eyes.

The Creator wants to have His humanity seeing in Creation. To be seeing, however, means to be knowing! And knowledge does not go with blind faith. Only indolence and slothful thinking lie in such a belief, not greatness!

The privilege of being endowed with the ability to think also brings man the duty to *investigate!*

In order to avoid all this, man out of laziness has simply so belittled the great Creator as to ascribe to Him arbitrary actions in proof of His Omnipotence.

He who will but think a little must again find a great error therein. An arbitrary act implies the possibility of diverting the existing Laws of Nature. However, where such a thing is possible, perfection is lacking. For where there is perfection there can be no alteration. Thus a large part of humanity erroneously represents the Omnipotence of God in such a way that those who think more deeply would have to regard it as a proof of imperfection. And therein lies the root of much evil.

Give God the honour of perfection! Then you will find the key to the unsolved riddles of all life. –

It shall be my endeavour to bring serious thinkers to this point. A sigh of relief shall go through the circles of all seekers for the Truth. Finally they will joyfully recognise that there is no mystery, no gap in the entire course of world events. And then ... they will see clearly before them the road to ascent. They only need to follow it. –

In all Creation there is no justification whatever for mysticism! There is no room for it, because everything should lie clearly and without gaps before the human spirit, right back to its origin. Only what is *above* that will have to remain a most sacred mystery to every human spirit. Therefore it will never be able to grasp what is Divine. Not with the best will and the greatest knowledge. But in this inability to grasp what is Divine lies the *most natural* thing for man that one can think of; for as everyone knows, it is not possible for anything to go beyond the composition of its origin. Nor for the spirit of man either! A boundary is always set by the difference in composition. And the Divine is of an entirely different consistency from the spiritual, in which man originates.*

The animal, for instance, can never become a human being, however highly developed its soul may be. From its animistic substance there cannot possibly blossom forth the spiritual which brings forth the human spirit. In the composition of all animistic substance the spiritual basic species is missing. Man, who has issued from the spiritual part of Creation, can in turn never become Divine either, because the spiritual has not the nature of Divine substance. The human spirit may well be able to develop to the highest degree of perfection, but must nevertheless always remain *spiritual.* It can never go above itself into the Divine. Here again the different consistency naturally

---

* A still more extensive breakdown in regard to this will be given in later lectures.

forms the ever impassable limitation upwards. The World of Matter does not come into it at all here since it has no life of its own, but serves as a covering, motivated and formed by the spiritual and the animistic.

The mighty field of the spirit extends through all Creation. Therefore man can, should and must fully grasp and recognise Creation! And through his knowledge he will rule therein. But rightly understood, to rule, however severely, simply means to serve! –

At no point in the entire Creation, up to the highest spiritual, is there any deviation from the natural happening! This fact alone surely makes all things much more familiar to everyone. The unhealthy and secret fear, the reluctance to face so many things as yet unknown, thus fall away of their own accord. With *naturalness* a fresh breeze blows through the sultry atmosphere formed by the morbid imaginings of those who like to cause a great stir. Their sickly fantastic creations, which terrify the weak and are mocked by the strong, have an absurd and childishly foolish effect on the sight that is becoming clear, and that finally, joyful and happy, takes in the glorious naturalness of every happening, which always moves only in simple straight lines that can be clearly recognised.

It runs through everything uniformly, in the strictest regularity and order. And this makes it easier for every seeker to obtain the broad, free view right to the point of his actual origin!

For this he needs neither painstaking research nor imagination. The main thing is for him to stand aloof from all those who in their muddled secretiveness try to make a scanty part-knowledge appear greater.

It all lies *so* simply before men that owing to the very simplicity they often do not come to recognition, because from the outset they assume that the great work of Creation must be much more difficult and intricate.

Here in spite of the best volition thousands stumble, they raise their eyes seekingly to the heavens, not realising that without effort they have only to look *before* and around them. They will then see that through their existence on earth they are already standing on the right road, and need only go calmly ahead! Without haste and without effort, but with *open* eyes and a free, unprejudiced mind! Man must at last learn that true greatness lies only in the most simple and natural happening. That greatness implies this simplicity.

So is it in Creation, so also in himself, who belongs to Creation as a part of it!

Only *simple* thinking and intuitive perceiving can give him clarity! Such simplicity as children still possess! Calm reflection will show him that, in the ability to comprehend, simplicity is identical with clarity and also with naturalness! The one simply cannot be thought of without the others. They form a triad that expresses *one* concept! Whoever makes it the foundation-stone of his search will soon break through the nebulous confusion. Everything that has been added artificially will then collapse into nothingness.

Man will realise that the natural order of events may nowhere be eliminated, and that at no place is it interrupted! And therein the greatness of *God* also reveals itself! The unchangeable vitality of the self-acting Creative Will! For the Laws of Nature are the inexorable Laws of God, continually visible to all men, appealing to them, testifying to the Greatness of the Creator, of an unshakable regularity, admitting of no exception! Of no exception! For a grain of oats can again bring forth only oats, likewise a grain of wheat only wheat, and so forth.

So is it also in that first Creation, which as the Creator's own Work stands nearest to His Perfection. There the fundamental Laws are anchored in such a way that, driven by the vitality of the Will, they were bound in the most natural order of events to result in the coming into being of the further Creation, right down finally to these celestial globes. Only becoming coarser the further Creation draws away in the process of development from the Perfection of the origin. –

Let us first of all just consider Creation.

Imagine that all life therein, no matter in what part it is found, is of two kinds only. The one kind is self-conscious and the other unconscious of itself. It is of the utmost value to observe these two different categories! This is connected with the "origin of man". The differences also give the stimulus to further development, to the apparent struggle. The unconscious is the basis of all the conscious, but its composition is of exactly the same nature. To become conscious is progress and development for the unconscious, which through association with the conscious is continually being stimulated also to attain to this consciousness.

In the process of developing downwards, the first Creation itself brought successively three great basic divisions: As uppermost and highest is the *spiritual*, the Primordial Creation, followed by the denser and thus also gradually heavier Sphere of Animistic Substance. Lastly as the lowest, and because of its greatest density the heaviest, still follows the great Realm of Matter which, severing itself from Primordial Creation, has gradually sunk down! Through this there finally remained as the uppermost only the Primordial Spiritual Substance, because in its pure nature it embodies what is lightest and most luminous. It is the oft-mentioned Paradise, the crown of all Creation.

With the sinking down of that which becomes denser we already touch upon the Law of Gravitation, which is not only anchored in matter, but has an effect in all Creation, from the so-called Paradise down to us.

The Law of Gravitation is of such decisive importance that everyone should hammer it into his mind; for it is the main lever in the whole evolution and process of development of the human spirit.

I have already said that this gravitation applies not only to earthly consistencies, but also works uniformly in those parts of Creation which earthmen can no longer see, and which they therefore simply call the beyond.

For a better understanding I must still divide the *World of Matter* into two sections. Into *ethereal matter* and *gross matter*. Ethereal matter is that matter which cannot become visible to the physical eye, owing to its different nature. And yet it still is matter.

The so-called "beyond" must not be confused with the longed-for Paradise, which is purely spiritual. The spiritual must not be taken as something "to do with thoughts", but the spiritual is a *consistency*, just as the animistic and the material are each a consistency. Therefore now this ethereal matter is simply called the "beyond", because it lies beyond earthly vision. Gross matter, however, is this side, all that is earthly, which on account of its similar species becomes visible to our gross material eyes.

Man should get rid of the habit of regarding things that are invisible to him as also incomprehensible and unnatural. *Everything* is natural, even the so-called beyond, and Paradise, which is still an immense distance from it.

Now just as here our physical body is sensitive to its surroundings of a *homogeneous* nature, which it can therefore see, hear and feel, so is it exactly the same in those parts of Creation whose consistency is not like ours. The ethereal man in the so-called beyond feels, hears and sees only his homogeneous *ethereal* environment; the higher spiritual man again can only feel his *spiritual* environment.

Thus it happens that many an earth-dweller now and then already sees and hears also the Ethereal World with his ethereal body, which he bears within, before the separation from the gross material earthly body takes place through physical death. There is absolutely nothing unnatural in this.

Side by side and co-operating with the Law of Gravitation is also the no less valuable Law of Homogeneous Species.

I have already touched upon this in saying that one species can only recognise the same species. The proverbs: "Birds of a feather flock together", and "like father, like son" seem to have been sensed from the Primordial Law. Together with the Law of Gravitation it swings throughout Creation.

In addition to those already mentioned there is a third Primordial Law in Creation: The Law of Reciprocal Action. The effect of this Law is that man must reap what he has once sown, unconditionally. He cannot reap wheat where he sowed rye, nor clover where he sowed thistles. In the Ethereal World it is exactly the same. In the end he will not be able to reap kindness where he felt hatred, nor joy where he nourished envy!

These three fundamental Laws form the corner-stones of the Divine Will! They alone automatically work out reward or punishment for a human spirit, with inexorable justice! So incorruptibly, in the most wonderful delicate gradations, that the thought of a slightest injustice in the gigantic world happening becomes impossible.

The effect of these simple Laws brings every human spirit exactly to the place where, according to his inner attitude, he does belong. Any error here is impossible, because the manifestation of these Laws can only be set in motion by the *inmost* condition of a human being, which will, however, set it in motion without fail in every case! Thus to bring this about the spiritual power of the *intuitive perceptions* which is *in* man is needed as the lever! Nothing else has any effect. For this reason only the real *volition,* man's *intuitive perception,* is decisive for what develops for him in the world that is invisible to him, and which he must enter after his earthly death.

There neither pretence nor self-deception will help him. He must then unconditionally reap what he has sown through his *volition!* What is more, exactly according to the strength or weakness of his volition, it sets in motion to a greater or lesser degree the homogeneous currents of the other worlds, no matter whether they are hatred, envy or love. An absolutely natural process, of the greatest simplicity, and yet with the inexorable effect of adamantine justice!

He who tries to go seriously and deeply into these happenings in the be-

137

yond will recognise what incorruptible justice lies in this automatic working, and will see in this alone the inconceivable Greatness of God. He does not need to interfere, after having given His Will as Laws, thus perfect, into Creation.

He who in the course of his ascent again enters the Spiritual Realm is purified; for he had first to pass through the self-acting mills of the Divine Will. No other road leads to the proximity of God. And *how* these mills work on the human spirit depends on its former inner life, its own *volition*. They can carry it blissfully into the Luminous Height; or on the other hand they can also pull it agonisingly down into the night of horror, indeed even drag it to complete destruction. –

It should be realised that at the time of its earthly birth the human spirit which has matured to the point of incarnation already wears an ethereal cloak or body, which it has needed on its journey through the Ethereal World. During its earthly existence this also remains with it as a connecting link to the physical body. Now the Law of Gravitation always exerts its main effect upon the densest and coarsest part. Thus during life on earth upon the physical body. But when this dies and falls away, the ethereal body again becomes free, and in this moment, being unprotected and now the coarsest part, is subject to this Law of Gravitation.

When it is said that the spirit forms its body, that is true as regards the ethereal body. The inner quality of man, his desires and his actual volition lay the foundation for it.

In the volition lies the power to form ethereal matter. Through the urge for what is base or for mere earthly pleasures the ethereal body becomes dense, and therewith heavy and dark, because the fulfilment of such desires lies in the World of Gross Matter. Thereby man binds himself to what is coarse and earthly. His desires draw along the ethereal body, that is to say, it is formed so densely that its consistency resembles as nearly as possible that of the earthly body. This alone holds the prospect of being able to participate in earthly pleasures or passions, as soon as the physical body has fallen away. Whoever strives after such things must sink through the Law of Gravitation.

But it is different with those people whose minds are mainly directed towards higher and nobler things. Here the volition automatically makes the ethereal body lighter and thus also more luminous, so that it can draw near to what to these human beings is the goal of their earnest aspirations! That is, to the purity of the Luminous Height.

Expressed in other words: Through the prevailing goal of the human spirit, the ethereal body in earthman is at the same time so equipped that after the death of the physical body it can strive towards this goal, whatever kind it may be. Here the spirit really forms the body; for its volition, being spiritual, also bears within it the power to make use of ethereal substance. The spirit can never evade this natural process. It happens with every volition, no matter whether it is pleasant or unpleasant for the spirit. And these forms remain clinging to it as long as the spirit nourishes them through its volition and intuition. They advance or retard the spirit according to their nature, which is subject to the Law of Gravitation.

Yet the moment the spirit changes its volition and intuition new forms will thereby immediately arise, whereas the old ones, no longer receiving nourishment because of this change, must fade and dissolve. In this way man also changes his fate.

Now as soon as the earthly anchorage falls away through the death of the physical body, the ethereal body which is thereby released either sinks down or floats up like a cork in the Ethereal World, which is called the "beyond". Through the Law of Gravitation it will be held fast exactly in that place which corresponds with its own weight; for then it cannot move further, either up or down. Here it will naturally also find all homogeneous species or all like-minded people; for like nature implies like weight, and like weight of course like nature. According to how man was himself, so will he have to suffer or be able to rejoice among those of like nature, until he changes anew inwardly, and with him his ethereal body, which under the effect of the altered weight must either lead him further upwards or downwards.

Therefore man can neither complain nor need he give thanks; for if he is raised towards the Light it is his own consistency that inevitably causes him to be raised; if he falls into the Darkness, it is again his condition that forces him to do so.

But every human being has reason to glorify and praise the Creator for the perfection that lies in the working of these three Laws. The human spirit is thereby unreservedly made the absolute master of its own fate! For its true volition, thus the genuine inner condition, must cause it either to rise or to sink.

If you try to get a true picture of the effect of these Laws, singly and working together, you will find that they contain reward and punishment, mercy or also damnation, minutely weighed for each one according to his inner state. It is the most simple process, and shows the lifeline provided by every serious volition of a human being, which can never break and never fail. It is the greatness of such simplicity that forcibly drives him who recognises to his knees before the infinite Sublimity of the Creator!

In every happening and in all my explanations we always again and again meet clearly and distinctly the effect of these simple Laws, whose wonderful interaction I must yet describe especially.

Once man knows this interaction he thus also has the step-ladder to the Luminous Realm of the Spirit, to Paradise. But he then also sees the road that leads down to the Darkness!

He need not even tread these steps himself, but the automatic mechanism raises him on high or drags him down, entirely according to how he adjusts the mechanism for himself through his *inner* life.

Which way he wishes to let himself be borne along is always left to *his* decision.

Man must not allow himself to be confused by scoffers.

Rightly viewed, doubt and derision are nothing but the expression of wishes. Quite unconsciously every doubter expresses what he wishes for himself, thus exposing his inner self to the searching glance. For denial and defence also harbour deeply hidden wishes which can be easily recognised. It is sad, or even revolting, to see what negligence or poverty of mind is thus sometimes revealed, because just through this a man often drags himself inwardly down below the level of any ignorant animal. One should have compassion for such people without, however, being indulgent; for indulgence would indeed mean cultivating indolence in serious investigation. He who seeks earnestly must become sparing with indulgence; otherwise he will ultimately harm himself without helping the other thereby.

But with growing recognition man will jubilantly stand before the wonder of such a Creation, and consciously let himself be borne aloft to the Luminous Heights which he may call his home!

THE HUMAN WORD

As a great grace for your maturing in the coarse World of Matter, the ability to form words has been bestowed upon you human beings by the Creator! You have never recognised the true value of this sublime gift, because you did not trouble yourselves about it, and treated it carelessly. Now you must suffer bitterly under all the consequences of your wrongdoing.

You stand in this affliction, and do not yet know the *causes* which bring such suffering in their wake.

No one may trifle with gifts of the Almighty without harming himself; such is the Law which rests and works in Creation, and which can never be diverted.

And when you consider that this being able to speak, thus your ability to form words, which anchor your volition in the World of Gross Matter through speaking, is an especially high gift of your Creator, then you will also know that it involves obligations for you, and that an immense responsibility arises therefrom; for it is with the language, and through it, that you are to work in Creation!

The words you form, the sentences, shape your outward fate on this earth. They are like seed in a garden which you build around you; for each human word is part of the most vital thing that *you* can weave for yourselves in this Creation.

Today I give you this, with an admonition, to think it over: there is a releasing quality in every word, because all words are firmly anchored in the Primordial Laws of Creation!

Every word shaped by man has come into being under the pressure of higher Laws and, according to its application, must manifest formingly in a very definite way!

The *application* lies in man's hands according to his free volition; however he is unable to control the effect, which is strictly and justly governed in conformity with the Holy Law by a power hitherto unknown to him.

Therefore in the final reckoning woe will now fall upon every human being who has abused the mysterious working of the word!

But where is *the* man who has *not* yet sinned in this respect! For thousands of years the whole earthly race has been deeply entangled in this guilt. What harm has already been spread throughout this earth by the wrong application of this gift of being permitted to speak!

Through ruinous, thoughtless and idle talk all men have sown poison. The seed has duly sprung up, the plant has blossomed forth, and now bears the fruit which you must harvest, whether you like it or not; for it is all the consequences of *your* actions that are now thrown into your lap!

That this poison *must* bring forth the most repulsive fruits will not surprise anyone who knows the Laws in Creation, which do not conform to the ideas of men, but serenely pursue their great course, irresistibly, without deviation, from the primordial beginning, and also unchanged unto all eternity.

Look around you, men, clearly and without bias: You *must* easily recognise the self-acting Divine Laws of the Most Holy Will, because you do have before you the fruits of your sowing! Wherever you look you will find that today high-sounding talk predominates and leads in everything. This seed *had* to come swiftly to such flower, to reveal now in the ripening its true kernel, whereby it will then collapse as useless.

It *had* to ripen under the increased pressure from the Light, and must shoot up as if in a hothouse; so that, losing every support through its hollowness, it will fall and bury all who with light-hearted confidence or selfish hope imagined themselves safe under its protection.

The time of harvest has already begun! Therewith all the consequences of wrong speaking now fall back upon the individual, as upon the entire masses who encouraged such talk.

It is quite *natural,* and shows the strict consistency of the effects of the Divine Laws, that now on the eve of the harvest the greatest talkers must in the end also gain the strongest influence and greatest power, as culmination and fruit of this continual wrong use of the word, whose mysterious working foolish humanity could no longer know, because they have long since closed themselves to the knowledge of it.

They did not listen to the warning voice of Jesus, the Son of God, Who already at that time said:

"Let your communication be yea or nay; for whatsoever is more than these cometh of evil!"

There is more in these words than you imagined; for they hold upbuilding or decline for mankind!

Through your propensity for much and useless talk you have chosen *decline,* which has already come to you. Finally, before the general collapse in the Judgment, it also still shows you quite clearly, as a help towards the saving recognition, all the fruits which you have forcibly brought into being through the wrong application of the word.

The reciprocal power now raises the masters at your own sins to the top, in such a way that you are in danger of being crushed by them, so that through recognition you will at last free yourselves from or be destroyed by them.

That *is* at the same time justice and help, as only the Will of God in His Perfection can offer you!

Just look around you! You *must* recognise it, if only you will. And for those who still hesitate to do so, the veil which they themselves hold before their eyes will yet be forcibly torn away from the fruits of their volition through still greater suffering than in the past, so that this earth may be cleansed from the pressure of your great guilt!

The entire mankind has actively participated in this, not merely individuals. They are the blossoms of all the wrongdoing over past centuries, which now had to ripen in these last fruits for the Judgment, so as to perish in this ripeness.

The frivolous, senseless and thoughtless chatter which, however, is always wrong and out of harmony with the Primordial Laws of Creation, had to culminate in the *universal* disease which is evident today, and must now in fever spasms, as in a storm, also shake off the fruits ... they drop into the lap of mankind.

Hence no people should be pitied who must now groan and suffer under this; for these are the fruits of their *own* volition, which must be consumed even if they taste rotten and bitter and bring destruction to many, because from poisonous seed only poison can be harvested. I have already said: where you sow thistles, no wheat can grow!

Thus out of agitation, mockery and harming your fellow-men there can never come any upbuilding whatever; for each kind of expression and attitude can only bring forth something *similar*, can only attract what is homogeneous! You must *never* forget this Law of Creation! It works *automatically*, and all human volition can never act against it! Never, do you hear that? Impress it upon yourselves, so that you may always heed it in your thinking, speaking and acting; for everything germinates from this and grows into your fate! Therefore never hope for anything else as fruit than always and only the same kind as the seed!

This after all is not so difficult, and yet it is just in this that you continually fail! Slander can again only produce slander, hate only hate, and murder only murder. But dignity, peace, light and joy can in turn only arise from a *dignified* way of thinking, never otherwise.

Liberation and redemption do not lie in the clamour of individuals and of the masses. A people that permits itself to be led by talkers must inevitably and rightfully fall into bad repute, into sorrow and death, into distress and misery; it is forcibly pushed into the mire.

And if hitherto the fruit and the harvest have so often not appeared in *one* earth-life, but only in later ones, this is now different; for the fulfilment of the Holy Will of God enforces *immediate* release of every happening on earth, and therewith also the unravelling of all the fates of men and of the peoples! Final reckoning!

Therefore guard your word! Pay careful attention to your speech; for the human word is also a deed which, however, can only produce forms in the Plane of Fine Gross Matter, that sink into and have an effect on everything earthly.

Yet do not imagine that promises are fulfilled according to their wording and thus grow into deeds, unless at the same time the speaker bears the *purest* intentions in his soul; but the words form *that* which from out of the *innermost being of the speaker* simultaneously vibrates with them. So the same word can produce two kinds of results, and woe unto him with whom it did not truthfully vibrate in complete purity!

I lift the veil covering your ignorance which has prevailed up to now, so that you may henceforth consciously experience the evil consequences, and benefit from them for the future.

As a further help I therefore give you:

Heed your word! Let your speech be simple and true! In accordance with the Holy Will of God, it contains an ability to form in an upbuilding or also in a destroying way, depending on the nature of the words and of the speaker.

Do not squander these sublime gifts which God so mercifully granted you, but seek to recognise them aright in their full value. Up till now the power of speech has been a curse to you through such people, who as Lucifer's satellites have misused it under the evil influence of the distorted and one-sidedly developed intellect!

Therefore beware of people who talk much; for with these goes disintegration. *You,* however, are to become *upbuilding ones* in this Creation, not talkers!

Heed your word! Do not talk merely for the sake of talking. And speak only when, where and how it is necessary! In the human word there shall be a reflection of the splendour of the Word of God, which is Life and will eternally remain Life.

You know that all Creation swings in the Word of the Lord! Does this not make you think? Creation vibrates in Him, as also do you yourselves, who are indeed part of Creation; for it arose out of Him and is maintained through this Word.

It has been clearly proclaimed to mankind:

"In the beginning was the Word! And the Word was with God! And the Word was *God!"*

Herein lies all knowledge for you, if you would only draw it. But you skim over it and do not heed it. Plainly it tells you:

The Word came *out of* God! It was and is a part out of Him.

A faint reflection of the power of the *Living* Word of God, which contains all and embraces all that is outside of God, a faint reflection of this also lies in the *human word!*

It is true that the human word is only able to send out its effect into the Planes of Fine Gross Matter, but that is enough retroactively to shape the destinies of men and also of peoples *here on earth!*

Remember that! He who talks much stands only on the ground of the distorted, one-sidedly developed intellect! The two always go hand in hand. By that you can recognise it! And these are words emanating from the low earthly planes, that can never build up. Yet in accordance with the Divine Law the word *is* to build up. Wherever it does not obey this command it can only bring about the opposite.

145

Therefore always heed your word! And *stand* to your word! You have still to be taught the right way to do this in the building up of the Kingdom of God here on earth.

You must first learn to recognise the power of the words which you have hitherto so thoughtlessly and frivolously debased.

Just think for once of the most Holy Word that has been given to you, of the Word: GOD!

You very often speak of God, *too* often for *that* awe still to resound in It which would indicate the right *intuitive perception* when you utter this Word: the awe which will allow you only to *whisper* the Sublime Word in reverential devotion, so as to shield It carefully from any kind of desecration.

But what have you men made of the most Sacred of all concepts in the Word! Instead of humbly and joyfully preparing your spirit for this most Sublime Expression, so that it may gratefully open itself to an unspeakable Radiation-Power of the Unsubstantiate Light-Sublimity of real Being, Who first permits you as well as all creatures to breathe, you have dared to drag It down to the low planes of your most trivial thinking, using It carelessly as an every-day word, which thereby had now to form itself in your ears into only an empty sound, and thus can find no entrance to your *spirit*.

It is then obvious that the effect of this most Sublime of all words will be different from the effect on those who whisper It with the proper awe and recognition.

Therefore pay attention to *all* words; for they hold joy or sorrow for you, they build up or disintegrate, they bring clarity but can also confuse, according to the manner *in which* they are spoken and applied.

I will later also give you recognition *for this*, so that you can *give thanks* with *every* word which the Creator still permits you to speak now! Then you shall also have earthly happiness, and peace will reign here on this hitherto troubled earth.

THE WOMAN OF SUBSEQUENT CREATION

THESE words touch upon the sorest spot in Subsequent Creation. *That* spot which needs the greatest change, the most lasting purification.

Although man of Subsequent Creation has made himself the slave of his own intellect, woman has transgressed to a far greater extent.

Equipped with the greatest delicacy of intuitive perceptions, she should easily swing herself up to the purity of Luminous Heights, and form the bridge to Paradise for all humanity. *Woman!* Streams of Light should flow through her. Her entire physical, gross material nature is adapted to this. Woman only needs to will honestly, and all the offspring from her womb *must* be strongly protected and encompassed by the power of the Light even before birth! It could not possibly be otherwise, because every woman through the wealth of her intuitive perception can almost entirely alone influence the spiritual nature of the fruit! Therefore she remains *primarily* responsible for all her descendants!

In addition she has been richly endowed with unlimited possibilities to influence the entire people, indeed even the whole of Subsequent Creation. Her starting-point of the greatest power is, for her, home and hearth! There alone lies her strength, her unlimited might, but not in public life! In home and family her abilities make her queen. From the quiet, intimate home her incisive virtue extends through the whole people, present and future, and pervades everything.

There is nothing upon which her influence cannot absolutely be brought to bear, if she stands *in that place* where her inherent *womanly* abilities fully unfold to blossom. But only if woman is truly *womanly* does she fulfil the mission which is assigned to her by the Creator. Then she is completely what she can and should be. And it is only genuine womanliness that silently educates the man who, supported by this quiet activity containing undreamed-of power, feels like storming the heavens. Out of an inner naturalness he will then gladly and joyfully seek to protect true womanhood as soon as it only shows itself to be *genuine.*

But womankind of today trample underfoot their real power and their high mission, they blindly overlook them, wantonly destroy all the sacred gifts they carry within them, and instead of being an upbuilding influence they bring about disintegration, thus being the most poisonous element in Subsequent Creation. They push man as well as children down with them into the abyss.

Look at the woman of today! Just let a ray of Light fall upon her with all the relentlessness and dispassion which are always accompanying conditions of Purity.

You will hardly recognise the high qualities of genuine womanhood, those in which there can be unfolded that pure might which is given only to the finer sensitiveness of womanhood, to be used solely as a *blessing*.

A man can never develop this pervading nature. The silent weaving of that invisible power which the Creator allows to move through the Universe, *first* and completely seizes *the woman* with her more delicate intuitive perception. Man receives it only partially, and then converts it into deeds.

And just as the Living Power of the Creator remains invisible to all men, while yet upholding, nourishing, moving and driving the whole Universe, *so* the weaving of all genuine womanhood is intended to be; it is *that for* which she has been created, and *that* is her high, pure and wonderful goal!

It is ridiculous to use the expression "weak woman", for woman is psychically stronger than man. Not in herself, but through being more closely connected with the Creative Power, which grants her the more delicate intuitive faculty.

And this is just what the woman tries to hide today; she exerts herself to coarsen or suppress it altogether. In boundless vanity and stupidity she surrenders the most beautiful and valuable gift bestowed on her. Through this she makes herself an outcast from the Light, to whom the way back will remain closed.

What has thereby become of these images of queenly womanhood! One must turn away from them with horror. Where does one still find in the woman of today the genuine feeling of shame, which is the expression of the most delicate intuitive perception of *noble* womanhood. It is so grossly distorted that is must be exposed to ridicule.

The woman of today is certainly ashamed to wear a long dress if fashion decrees a short one, but she is not ashamed to expose almost three-quarters of her body, offering it to the glances of all on festive occasions. And of course not only to their glances but also, when dancing, unavoidably to their hands! Without hesitation she would also uncover still more if fashion required it, probably even everything judging by present experiences!

This is no exaggeration. For hitherto we have had enough of this disgraceful conduct. It was not a wrong but, alas, only too true a saying that "woman begins to *dress* herself when she retires for the night"!

Besides, delicate intuitive perceptions also demand a sense of beauty! Unquestionably. But if today the delicacy of womanly intuitive perceptions is still to be assessed on that basis, then affairs are in a deplorable state. Indeed, the type of dress often and plainly enough tells the opposite, and these thinly-stockinged legs of a woman, or even of a mother, are very difficult to reconcile with womanly dignity. Bobbed hair and modern sports for women are no less harmful to genuine womanhood! Coquetry is the inevitable accompaniment of vain fashion follies, which result in grave dangers for body and soul, to say nothing of the simple domestic happiness. Often enough many a woman prefers the coarse and really insulting flattery of some idler to the faithful labour of her husband.

Thus much, very much more could be cited as visible evidence that a woman of today is lost to her *real* task in this Subsequent Creation! And likewise all the high values entrusted to her, of which she must now give an account. Accursed be these empty human beings! They are not the victims of circumstances, but they have forced these circumstances into being.

All this talk about progress does not alter the fact that these zealots of progress, together with their faithful followers, only sink deeper, ever deeper. Already they have all buried their real values. The majority of womankind no longer deserve to bear the name of honour, woman! And they can never represent nor become men, thus in the end they remain nothing but drones in Subsequent Creation, which must be exterminated according to the inflexible Laws of Nature.

Of all the creatures in Subsequent Creation, woman stands least in the place where she should stand! In her way she has become the saddest figure among all creatures! She simply *had* to become corrupt in soul, since she wantonly sacrifices her most noble intuitive perception, her purest power, to outward, absurd vanity, thereby ridiculing and scorning the decree of her Creator. With such superficiality there can be no salvation; for these women

149

would reject words, or be no longer able to understand and grasp them at all.

Thus out of the horrors the new, true woman must first arise, who has to become the mediator, and therewith also provide the foundation for the new God-willed life and human activity in Subsequent Creation, the woman who will have become free from poison and corruption!

SUBMISSION

"THY WILL be done!" People who believe in God utter these words submissively! But a certain sadness always vibrates in their voices or lies in their thoughts, in their intuitive perceptions. These words are used almost exclusively where *sorrow* that was *inescapable* has entered. Where man realises that he could do nothing more about it.

Then, if he is a believer, he will say in passive submission: *"Thy Will be done!"*

It is not humility, however, that prompts him to speak thus, but the words are meant to calm him in face of something he has been powerless to deal with.

That is the origin of the submission which man expresses in such a case. If, however, he were offered the slightest opportunity to alter things in any way, he would not care about the Will of God, but his submissive attitude would again quickly be changed to the form: *"My will be done!"*

Such is man! – – –

"Do with me as Thou wilt, O Lord!" and similar hymns are often to be heard at funerals. But every mourner bears within him the unshakable wish: "If I could alter it I would do so at once!"

Human submission is *never* genuine. Deeply implanted in a human soul lies the opposite. Rebellion against the fate that befalls it; and it is this very protest that causes the soul's suffering, which "oppresses" and bows it down.

What is unhealthy in this is due to the wrong application of the meaning of these words: "Thy Will be done!" They do not belong where man and churches use them.

The Will of God lies in the Laws of this Creation! Whenever man says: "Thy Will be done!" it is tantamount to affirming: "I will honour and obey Thy Laws in Creation!" To honour means to *observe* them, but to observe them demands to live accordingly! Only thus can man honour the Will of God!

151

But if he wants to observe It, if he wants to live accordingly, he must also first of all *know* It!

That is just the point, however, against which mankind on earth has transgressed in the worst way! Until now man has never concerned himself with the Laws of God in Creation! Thus not with the Holy Will of God! And yet he utters over and over again: "Thy Will be done!"

You see how unthinkingly earthman approaches God! How senselessly he seeks to apply the sublime words of Christ. Plaintively, often writhing in anguish, feeling himself defeated, but never with a joyful pledge!

"Thy Will be done" actually means: "I will act according to It" or "I desire Thy Will!" One can just as well also say: "I will obey Thy Will!"

But he who obeys also *acts*. One who obeys is not inactive; that is implied in the very word. He who obeys also *does something.*

Yet as the man of *today* says: "Thy Will be done!" he wishes *to do nothing himself,* but puts into his intuitive perception the meaning: "I remain still, *You do it!"*

He considers himself great in this, believing that he has conquered himself and "become merged" with the Will of God. Man even imagines himself superior to all others thereby, and believes he has made a tremendous advance.

All such people, however, are useless weaklings, idlers, enthusiasts, visionaries and fanatics, but no useful links in Creation! They are numbered among those who must be rejected in the Judgment; for they do not want to be *labourers* in the vineyard of the Lord! The humility of which they boast is nothing but indolence. They are idle servants!

The Lord demands *life,* which lies in *movement! –*

Submission! This word should not exist at all for believers in God! Simply replace it with "joyful volition"! God does not want dull submission from men, but joyful activity.

Just look closely at those who are described as "resigned to God's Will". They are hypocrites who bear a great lie within them!

Of what use is it to cast a glance of submissive resignation upwards, if at the same time man looks around with cunning, lust, arrogance, conceit or malice! This only makes him *doubly* guilty.

Submissive people bear the lie within, for submission is absolutely incompatible with "spirit"! Therefore also with a human spirit! All that is "spirit" is utterly unable to bring the quality of true submissiveness to life within itself! Wherever it is attempted it must remain artificial, thus self-delusion or even conscious hypocrisy! But it can never be genuinely felt because the human spirit, being spiritual, is incapable of it. The pressure under which the human spirit stands does not allow the quality of submissiveness to become conscious. The pressure is too strong for this. And therefore man cannot practise it either.

Submissiveness is a quality that lies solely in the animistic! Only in the animal does it find genuine expression. The *animal* is submissive to its master! But the spirit does not know this designation! Therefore it *always* remains unnatural for the human being.

Submission was drilled into slaves with difficulty and harshness, because they were put on a par with animals in sale and purchase, as personal property. Yet the submission could never become really genuine in these slaves. It was either dullness, fidelity or love that lay hidden under the submission and gave it expression, but never true submission. Slavery is unnatural among men.

The submission of the animistic finds its enhancement in the spiritual in conscious and willed loyalty! What denotes submission in the animistic, therefore, is loyalty in the spiritual!

Submission does not befit man; because he is of the spirit! Just pay closer attention to the language itself, which indeed expresses in its words what is right, and bears the true meaning in it. It gives you the right picture.

For instance, the victor also says to the vanquished: "Submit!" In this word lies the meaning: "Surrender yourself to me unconditionally so that I may deal with you as I see fit, even over life or death!"

But in this the victor acts wrongly; for even in victory man has to conform strictly to the Laws of God. Otherwise with every neglect of them he makes himself guilty before the Lord. The reciprocal action will then strike him without fail! This applies to the individual as well as to entire peoples!

And now the time has come when everything, everything that has hitherto taken place in the world, must be redeemed! What has been wrong, what is happening on earth *today, not one word will remain unatoned for!*

The atonement is not reserved for a distant future, but is already taking place in the *present time!*

Thus the *speedy* release of *all* the reciprocal actions is not opposed to the Law of Creation, but lies quite correctly in the Law itself.

The action of the mechanism is at present accelerated by the increased radiation of the Light, which enforces final effects by first driving everything to fruition and over-ripeness, so that the false will decay therein and in withering away judge itself, while the good will become free from the hitherto existing pressure of the wrong and can gain strength!

In the near future this radiation will be so intensified that in very many cases the reciprocal action will come *at once, instantaneously!*

This is the power which will soon alarm earthmen, and which they will then have to fear in the future! But only *those* who have done *wrong* need fear it, and rightly so. Whether they have thought themselves in the right, or have tried to make others believe they were, it will not save them from the blow of the reciprocal effect that operates in the Laws of God!

Even though men have devised different laws on earth, under whose protection many act wrongly and unjustly in the delusion that they are thereby also in the right, it does not absolve them of one particle of their guilt.

The Laws of God, thus the Will of God, do not concern themselves with the opinions of these earthmen, which they have laid down in their mundane laws, even though the whole world has now considered them to be right. Whatever is not in harmony with the Divine Laws, there also the blow of the sword will now strike! Judging in the process of redemption!

All those who in the light of God's Laws have suffered *innocently* at the hands of men may now rejoice; for henceforth they shall receive justice, while their adversaries or judges are delivered up to the Justice of God.

Rejoice; for this Divine Justice is near! It is already working in every country on earth! Look at the confusion! This is the effect of the *approaching* Will of God! It is the setting-in of the purification!

For this reason everything that is wrong among men is already *now* meeting with its doom, be it in economics, the state, politics, the churches, sects, peoples, families and also in the individual! Everything, everything is now dragged before the Light, *so that it may reveal and simultaneously judge itself therein!* Also what has hitherto been able to remain hidden *must* reveal itself as it *really* is, must become active, and thus finally, despairing of itself and others, disintegrate and turn to dust.

Thus even now there is a boiling up under the pressure of the Light in all countries, everywhere. Every kind of tribulation is increasing to the point of despair, until finally nothing remains but hopelessness, with the realisation that the would-be saviours had *only empty words* besides selfish desires, but could offer no help! Spiritual warriors are sweeping over all humanity, and striking sharply where a head refuses to bow.

Only then will there be the right soil that pleads once more for *God's* help! After murder and fire, starvation, pestilence and death, after man has recognised his own incapacity.

The great upbuilding begins.

Then the despairing ones shall become free, free from the pressure of the Darkness! But they shall also become free *within themselves!* To become free within, however, can only be achieved by each individual *alone.* Yet for this he must know what freedom means, what it *is.*

Only the man who lives in the Laws of God is free! Thus and not otherwise does he stand unoppressed and unconstrained in this Creation. Everything then serves him instead of obstructing his path. It "serves" him because he uses it in the right way.

God's Laws in Creation are in truth simply all that every man needs for a healthy, happy life in Creation. They are, as it were, nourishment for his well-being! Only he who knows the Will of God and lives accordingly is really free! All the others must bind themselves in many threads of the Laws of this Creation, because they entangle themselves.

Creation originated only in the Will of God, in His Laws. Working together, the threads of these Laws sink deeper and deeper, everywhere enforcing movement towards development, and inevitably branching out more and more in the course of development, while in the continuous movement new creations are perpetually formed around the threads. Thus these Laws provide at the same time the support, the possibility of continued existence and the further expansion of Creation.

Nothing exists without this Will of God, Which alone gives movement. Everything in Creation conforms to It.

Only the human spirit has *not* adjusted itself to these threads! It has tangled them and thereby entangled itself, because it wanted to follow new roads according to *its* will, and disregarded those already prepared and in existence.

The increasing power of the Light is now changing this. The threads of all the Divine Laws in Creation are being charged with increased energy, so that they become powerfully taut. This enormous tension causes them to spring back into their original position. What is tangled and knotted is thereby disentangled, so suddenly and irresistibly that everything that cannot still adapt itself to the right position in Creation is simply torn down in this process!

Whatever it may be, whether plant or animal, whether mountains, streams, countries, states or man himself, all will collapse that cannot prove itself at the last moment to be genuine and willed by God!

THE COSMIC Clock can be heard on earth as it now booms out the hour of twelve through the Universe! Frightened, Creation holds its breath, and every creature bows down in fear; for the Voice of *God* rings down and demands! Demands that you render account, you who have been permitted to live in this Creation!

You have mismanaged the bounty which God in His Love made over to you. All those servants who have thought only of *themselves* and never of their Master will now be expelled! And all those who sought to make themselves the master. –

You men shy away from my words, for you do not consider severity Divine! But that is only *your* fault, because until now you have imagined everything Divine, everything that comes down from God, to be tenderly loving and all-forgiving, since that is what the churches have taught you!

But these false teachings were only intellectual schemes aimed at the mass-capture of human souls on earth. In order to catch something, a bait is needed that is attractive to everything at which it is aimed. The right choice of bait is the main thing for each catch.

Now as this was intended for *human souls*, a plan based on *their* weaknesses was skilfully devised. The lure had to correspond to the main weakness! And this main weakness of the souls was love of ease, the indolence of their spirit!

The church knew very well that it was bound to achieve great success as soon as it showed much leniency towards *this* weakness, and did not require it to be overcome!

Recognising this aright, it built for earthmen a broad and easy road that was ostensibly to lead to the Light, and displayed it enticingly to these earthmen who would prefer to give one-tenth of the fruits of their labour, go on their knees and murmur prayers by the hundred, rather than exert *themselves spiritually for even one moment!*

Therefore the church took the spiritual effort away from men, also pardoning all their sins if they were obedient outwardly and in the earthly sense, and carried out what *the church* required of them in mundane ways!

Whether in the way of church attendance, confessions, in the number of prayers, in tributes or in donations and bequests, no matter what, the *church* was satisfied. They left the believers under a delusion that everything they did for the *church* would also secure them a place in Heaven.

As if the church could allot these places!

However, the achievements and the allegiance of all believers links them only *with their church*, not with their God! Neither the church nor its servants can take away from or even forgive a human soul one particle of its guilt! Just as little are they permitted to canonise a soul, and thereby interfere in God's perfect eternal Primordial Laws of Creation, which are immutable!

How can *men* presume to vote and also to decide on matters that rest in the Omnipotence, the Justice and the Omniscience of God! How dare earthmen try to make their fellow-men believe such things! And it is no less sacrilegious for earthmen credulously to accept such claims, which so plainly carry within them only a dishonouring of the Sublimity of God!

Anything so incredible can only be possible with thoughtless people of herd mentality, who by such action brand themselves with the mark of the greatest spiritual indolence; for the most simple reflection must enable anyone instantly and easily to realise that such persumptions cannot even be explained by human conceit or arrogance, but contain grave blasphemies!

The reciprocal effect must be terrible!

The time of God's forbearance is now indeed over. Holy Wrath strikes the ranks of those offenders who thereby seek to dupe humanity on earth in order to increase and preserve their authority, whereas within themselves they clearly sense that here it is a question of matters far beyond the level to which they can ever be entitled to rise!

How dare they dispose of the Kingdom of God in Eternity? Overnight the Ray of Divine Wrath will awaken them from their unbelievable spiritual slumber and ... *judge* them! – – –

What does a man give to his God by obedience to the church! He does not have with it a single, *natural* intuitive urge, which alone can help him to ascend.

I say to you that men can in truth only serve God with just *that* which did *not* come to life through the churches: With their *own* thinking and *independent* investigation! Everyone must journey *alone* through the mills, through the mechanism of the Divine Laws in Creation. And therefore it is necessary for *every man himself* to become acquainted at the right time with the nature and function of the mills.

But this is just what many a church has persistently withheld, so that the believers could not develop the necessary *personal* reflection and intuitive perception. Thereby they robbed man of that staff which alone can guide him safely and direct him towards the Light, and tried instead to force upon every man an interpretation, the acceptance of which was bound to bring benefit only to the *church*. Benefit, influence and power!

Human souls can serve their Creator only by the *activity of their own spirit!* Thereby, however, in the first place they are also simultaneously serving themselves. Only *that* human spirit which stands bright and alert in this Creation, aware of its Laws and adapting itself to them in thought and deed, is pleasing to God, because it is then fulfilling the purpose of existence, which every human spirit has in this Creation!

But this never lies in the observances that the churches demand of their believers! For these lack naturalness and free conviction, knowledge, as the *main requisite* of true service to God! There is a lack of vigour and joy in helping all creatures to advance, in letting their souls exult in the happiness of knowing that they can contribute to the beauty of this Creation as a part of it, and *thereby* thank and honour the Creator!

Instead of joyful, free worshippers of God, the church has cultivated church-slaves for itself! It has thrust *itself* before men's free upward gaze! Thereby obscuring true Light. It has only bound and gagged the human spirits, instead of awakening and liberating them. Wantonly it has kept the spirits in slumber, oppressed them, restrained their desire for knowledge, and forbidden the knowledge itself through regulations that are contrary and opposed to the Will of God! All this in order to uphold its *own* power.

Even as in olden times the churches have not shrunk from various forms of torture, torment and murder, so today they do not hesitate to slander their fellow-men, speak ill of them, undermine their reputation, agitate against them, and put every available obstacle in their way if they are not willing to join the host of church-slaves! They work with the most sordid means only for *their* influence, *their* earthly power.

159

But through the reciprocal action this now will also be the very first to waver and collapse; for it is the opposite of what *God* wills! It shows how far removed they are from humbly serving *God!* –

Enticed by the sanctioned indolence of the spirit, endless multitudes have allowed themselves to be drawn into the fold of the church, which lulls them to sleep! They believed the wicked delusion of a cheap atonement for their sins, and as the spiritually indolent masses grew so did the earthly influence, with the final goal of earthly power! The people did not see that the false view and teaching obscured and defiled the Sacred Justice of Almighty God; they saw only the thus simulated broad and easy road to the Light, which in reality does not exist at all! Through its arbitrary, illusory forgiveness it leads to Darkness and destruction!

The self-glorification of all the churches, which is hostile to God, separates their believers from God instead of leading them to Him. The doctrines were false! But the people should easily have found this out *themselves,* for they clearly contradict the simplest sense of justice! And therefore the church believers are *just as guilty* as the churches themselves!

The churches proclaim in the words of Christ from the Gospel of John:

"Howbeit when he, the Spirit of truth, is come, he will guide you into all truth. And when he is come, he will reprove the world of sin, and of righteousness! And will bring the Judgment. I, however, go to the Father and you will henceforth not see me. I came forth from the Father and am come into the world. Again, I leave the world and go to the Father!"

These words are read in the churches without understanding; for it is quite clearly stated by the Son of God that *another* than He will come to proclaim the Truth and to bring the Judgment. The Spirit of Truth Who is the Living Cross! And yet in this matter, too, the church teaches wrongly and against these clear words.

Even though Paul also once wrote to the Corinthians: "For *we* know in part. But when that which is perfect is come, then that which is in part shall be done away!"

Here the Apostle shows that the coming of Him Who will proclaim the Perfect Truth is yet to be expected, and that the prophecy of the Son of God concerning it should not be taken to refer to the well-known outpouring of the Power of the Holy Spirit, which at that time had already taken place when Paul wrote these words.

He testifies thereby that the Apostles did *not* regard this outpouring of Power as the fulfilment of the mission of the Comforter, the Spirit of Truth, as strange to say many churches and believers now try to interpret it at Whitsuntide, because these things would not otherwise fit into the structure of their faith, but would form a gap which must cause serious shocks to this false edifice.

Yet it avails them nothing; for the time has come for the recognition of all these things, and everything that is false collapses!

Until now there could not yet be a true Pentecost for mankind; the recognition through spiritual awakening could not come to them, since they acquiesced in so many false interpretations, in which the churches especially have a great share!

Nothing of their great guilt will be remitted to them! –

Now you men stand amazed before the new Word, and many of you are no longer even capable of perceiving that It comes from the Luminous Heights, because It is so different from what you had imagined! For in you, too, there certainly still lives some of the tenacious indolence in which the churches and the schools have enveloped you, so that you would remain faithful followers, and have no longing for the awakening of your own spirit!

Until now men on earth have been indifferent to what *God* demands! Once more, however, I say to you: "The broad and easy road which the churches have hitherto tried to simulate for their own advantage is *wrong!* With its promise of an arbitrary, illusory forgiveness, it does not lead to the Light!"

MEN, WHAT has been your attitude towards your God up till now! Hypocritically you have sought to deceive Him, even as you have always wished to deceive yourselves with the false piety which was only lip-service, but never shared by your spirit. *You* have established rules and observances, in your temples, your churches, without asking whether this way was pleasing to *God*. If only they pleased *you,* then that settled the service to God for you!

Do you not see how arrogant all this was. *You* wanted to decide the way everything should be arranged. In doing so you have never cared about *God's* Will. What *you* termed great was to be equally acceptable to God. You wanted to force *your* opinions in all things upon God as justified, irrespective of what you were dealing with.

What *you* considered right was to be rewarded by God as righteous; what *you* chose to call wrong God was to punish.

You have never seriously wanted to find out what *God* regards as right, and what before *His* Eye is wrong. You have paid no attention to the Divine Laws, nor to the inexorable Holy Will of God, Which has existed from all Eternity and has never yet changed, nor ever will change!

It will now shatter you, and with you all the false works of man, which have created laws to serve *your earthly desires.* But you human beings yourselves stand before God as scheming, neglectful servants who in their selfishness, self-conceit and ridiculous claim to know everything have never respected *His* Will.

You have been and still are servants who thought themselves masters, and who out of arrogance and spiritual indolence have tried to resist and drag down all that they could not understand, if it did not agree with the attainment of the base earthly ends which they wished to be regarded as of the highest order.

You miserable ones, who could so transgress! Everything was only to serve *you, even the Laws!* Only what served you, regardless of its form, only what helped you towards the fulfilment of your earthly desires – only *that* did you acknowledge as right, only such things did you still want to know about.

But should it now be required of you that you yourselves should eagerly and loyally serve your Lord, to Whom you owe your existence, then you are quite astonished, since in your opinion it is only He Himself Who should serve you with His Power, with His Glory and His Great Love!

How could it possibly be *otherwise,* in view of the high opinion you have of yourselves! For you thought it was service enough to God if you acknowledge Him, and ask in thought for His help to fulfil all the wishes you carry within you. To put it plainly, that He should *serve you* with the Omnipotence that is His own, and make your life pleasant! Nothing else enters your mind.

At its best your service to God has been *begging!*

Just think it over very carefully for once; it has never yet been otherwise.

When you examine yourselves in this respect, are you not seized with both shame and anger about yourselves?

The majority of mankind think that the only object of this earth-life is the purpose of acquiring material gain! Also at best the purpose of a family and children! He who does not *think* so still *acts* accordingly! But on such a basis what is the use of propagation, as you call it, which in reality does not mean propagation at all, but simply provides opportunities for other human spirits to incarnate so that these may continue to improve themselves and cast off old faults. By your behaviour you add to the burden of your guilt; for you thereby prevent all those spirits from ascending, whom you bring up as your children for the same empty purposes!

What is the good of building up an earthly kingdom if it is not intended for the honour of God, if it does not work according to the Wishes of God, about Which you are still completely ignorant, and have hitherto not wanted to learn anything either, since *your* wishes are more important to you than anything else. You only want to satisfy *yourselves*, and then even expect God to bless your poor efforts! You do not care to serve and to fulfil your duty towards your God.

The strange activities of mankind on earth, who in their folly even dare to drag the Name of God into everything that is false, thereby defiling what is most sacred, will now be shattered!

You will be thrust from the throne of your intellectual artifice so that at least some of you may still become able, in pure humility, to receive true Wisdom from Divine Heights, Which alone can make you human beings; for you would never mature for this of your own accord.

What does not suit you, you slander, and you are quick to pick up stones to do away with anything that is irksome enough to disturb you from the continued belief in yourselves.

You would rather hail Luciferian satellites who, in flattering your vanities and encouraging your self-conceit, then all the more surely cut you off from the Light and keep you in spiritual indolence, which must lead to the sleep of death for your true being!

But I say to you that you are now awakened from the intoxication, the oppressive delirium, that is already holding you in its iron grip. You must awaken *against* your will, be it only to recognise with the most terrible despair, even at the last moment, all you have freely abandoned with such wanton indifference – before you are thrust into the bottomless pit that seems so desirable to you!

This earth and the whole world is now being purified! No longer shall any of the filth remain; so that the creatures will be able peacefully and joyfully to serve their Lord, the Almighty God, Who in His Love once granted them the conscious enjoyment of all the blessings of Creation.

He who again tries to bring disturbance into it by disregarding or even opposing the Laws of God in Creation will be mercilessly eliminated; for with such conduct he brings to you only envy, hate, suffering, disease and death!

All this tribulation can only still be avoided if you really seek to recognise and honour the *Word of the Most High!* To do so, however, It must first be understood in *Its true nature!* But hitherto you have always construed It only as It pleased *you!* And not as It was given by God for your help, your salvation, out of the greatest need!

However, you have not shrunk from making even the Holy Word the slave of your arrogance, so that through the distortion of Its true meaning It might serve only *you*; instead of *you* serving the Word for your own salvation in *that* sense in which It was given to you!

What have you made of the Word of God in your explanations, and even in the Scriptures! That you can quarrel about It, that you as human beings can come together and deliberate this way and that way over It, even this in itself is evidence of an unsound foundation and of a lack of clarity in what you have dared to set up as the pure, sublime Word of God! The Word of the Lord is inviolable, simple, clear and indestructibly hewn into Creation.

Where It is not obscured and distorted there can be no analysing, no deliberation! It is clear to *every* creature.

But for you, with your ridiculous conceit, the greatness of this simplicity was still too small! In the gloom of your mental workshop you have laboriously toiled away at the Word until you could distort and mould It *in such a way* that It pleased *you,* so that It conformed to your petty earthly desires, your weaknesses, and also to your great opinion of yourselves and your importance.

In this way you created something that had to serve you, that flattered your vanity.

For also that humility which you display when you speak of your great sins, for which a *God* brought the sacrifice of atonement, is nothing but the basest vanity. *A God for you!* How valuable you must imagine yourselves! And you need do nothing further about it than graciously condescend, after much persuasion, merely to ask for remission!

This train of thought must surely make even the most conceited feel somewhat uneasy in his hypocritical humility.

But this is only one thing among many. You have thus distorted *everything* that is intended to clarify your relation as a self-conscious creature towards the great Creator!

Nothing of it has remained pure and sublime under the conceit of this humanity on earth. Therefore the right attitude towards God has automatically changed and become false.

Presumptuously expecting a good reward or disdainfully begging, only *thus* have you stood before your Lord – if indeed you have ever taken the trouble and time really to think of Him, forced to do so by many a misfortune that had to strike you in the reciprocal effect of your actions!

But now you must at last awaken and must accept the Truth as It *really is,* not as *you* think It is! With this what is false collapses, and the gaps due to your hypocritical claim of knowing everything better become apparent. Nothing can hide in the Darkness any longer; for through the Will of God there will henceforth be Light, so that the Darkness will fall and perish!

Now there will be Light also on earth and in the whole great World of Matter! It blazes forth radiantly in every part, disintegrating and burning all evil as well as all evil volition. Everything false must show itself wherever it seeks to hide, must collapse of itself before the Ray of God's Light, which now illuminates the entire Creation! All that is not and does not wish to live in accordance with the Sublime Laws of God will sink down to the region of destruction, where it can never arise again! –

ALL THAT IS DEAD IN CREATION SHALL BE AWAKENED, SO THAT IT MAY PASS JUDGMENT UPON ITSELF!

THE DAY of Judgment! Every prophecy that is connected with this proclaims the resurrection of all the dead for the Final Judgment! But this mankind have again introduced an error into the concept of the expression; for it is not meant to denote: Resurrection of *all the* dead, but resurrection of *all that is* dead! That is: The animating of all that is without movement in Creation, so that it may become *alive* for the Divine Judgment, either to be strengthened in its activity or annihilated!

Today nothing remains motionless; for the Living Power that now flows with greater intensity through all Creation urges, presses and forces everything into motion. Thereby it grows stronger, including that which has hitherto been inactive or dormant. It is awakened, strengthened, and thus *must* become active; in this awakening activity it is, so to speak, dragged before the Light, even if it wished to hide. It can also be said that it comes to the Light of itself and must reveal itself; it can no longer remain dormant, wherever it may be. As the popular saying is: "It comes to light!"

Everything becomes life and activity in this entire Creation through the new penetration of the Light! The Light thereby exerts a powerful attraction ... whether that which rests or perhaps even hides in this Creation wishes it or not; and finally it will also come into contact with this Light, it cannot escape It, even if it had the wings of the morning no place in the entire Creation can grant it protection from the Light. There is nothing which will not be lit up.

But in the movement of being attracted, anything that cannot endure the radiation, thus anything that is not already voluntarily striving towards this Light, must be shattered and burnt up by the Light. What is attuned to the Light, however, will blossom and grow strong in the purity of its volition!

So is it also with all the *qualities* of the souls of these earthmen. What has hitherto appeared to be dead, what has slumbered in them, often unknown to men themselves, will awaken and become strong under the Power, will develop into thought and deed, so that according to its nature it will in manifesting judge itself by the Light! Reflect, whatever is slumbering *in you* will come to life! Therein lies the resurrection of all that is dead! The Living Judgment! The Day of Judgment!

Then you must deal with all that is within you, must purify yourselves, or you will perish with the evil if it is able to become too powerful in you. It will then *hold* you fast, break over your head with foaming and bubbling, to sweep you down with it into the abyss of disintegration; for it can no longer exist in the radiance of Divine Power! – –

To you I have now given the Word showing the way that, in the awakening of this Creation, leads you unerringly to the Luminous Heights, the way that will not let you fall, whatever happens and tries to flare up within you! If you have turned your gaze to the Light in loyal conviction, if you have rightly grasped my Word and absorbed it in your souls, then you will calmly ascend out of the chaos, cleansed and purified, free from everything that might once have hindered you from entering Paradise.

Watch and pray, therefore, that you do not let your clear outlook be dimmed by vanity and conceit, the most dangerous snares for these earthmen! Beware! As you have now prepared the soil within you, so will it happen to you during the purification of Creation! –

Even as the Darkness moved over Golgotha when Jesus, the Living Light, departed from this earth, so is it now moving over mankind, returning to them the great suffering they inflicted upon the Love of God in the cruel way of the cunning intellect, which is utterly incapable of any intuitive vibrations, and which as Lucifer's most powerful tool you have held sacred! –

Now try if you can, you human beings, to protect yourselves with your intellect against God's All-Holy Wrath! Defend yourselves against the Omnipotence of Him Who graciously made over for your use *that* part of Creation which you have devastated and defiled like a stable of the most neglected animals, so that only suffering and misery can still dwell therein, because all peace and joy flee before your wrong actions and dark volition, and all purity conceals itself in horror.

Try to hide from God's inflexible Justice! It strikes you *everywhere* in the inexorable execution of Divine Will, without remitting anything of the enormous guilt with which you have laden yourselves in your self-will and obstinacy.

You are judged even before you are able to stammer a single word of excuse, and all petitioning, all supplicating, all blaspheming or cursing avails you nothing; for now you have unpardonably wasted the last respite for searching your soul and turning back, merely on fostering your vices! –

I do not tell you this as a warning; because it is too late for that. Far be it from me to continue to admonish you as I have done for years. You are only to think of it in the coming *experiences!* For this reason I state once more what this time has in store for you. Perhaps the knowledge of it will help to *alleviate* many an affliction for you, although it can no longer prevent anything.

You know it is the clearing of the debt with which you have voluntarily burdened yourselves, since nobody has forced you to do this. If through my words you can come to recognition in the suffering, and if thereby a yearning for Light and for Purity arises within you and forms a humble petition, you may still be granted salvation as you are sinking; for God's Love is ever watchful.

Then you will also be permitted to see the new life, which the Lord will grant only to *those* who willingly swing in the sacred Laws of His Creation, to those who will keep His Mansion in which you are but guests free from all activities that are hostile to the Light, and who will not again wantonly devastate the beautiful gardens, in whose splendour and purity they shall evermore rejoice in order to grow strong therein.

Oh, you deluded ones, why would you not awaken! You could have been spared so much hardship. But as it is, your existence must be shrouded in grey veils of deep sorrow, from which only through the piercing flashes of the Holy Wrath of God can liberation and redemption once more be granted to you!

And this Wrath will break over you with unsuspected might in the Holy Judgment! –

But the Judgment is *different* from your conception of it. You know of a Book of Life which will be opened by the Judge of God at the appointed hour for *each* one!

The Book of Life shows *the names* of all creatures who have come to life, and nothing else.

But the inscribed pages belonging to the great Book of Life, which show the for and against of every single thought and every single deed of the individual, are *the souls themselves,* upon whom has been imprinted all that they have experienced or done in the course of their existence.

The Judge can clearly read *therein* all the for and against. But again you also picture the reading wrongly. This too is much simpler than you try to imagine.

The Judge does not order each soul to step separately before Him, before His Judgment Seat, but in the Name of God He sends His sword-thrusts *into the Universe!* The sword-thrusts are *radiations,* which go forth and strike *everything* in Creation!

Realise the great simplicity and amazing naturalness! The Judge does not send the rays consciously or intentionally to this one or that one; no, He simply sends them *out* at God's Holy Command; for it is the Power of *God,* nothing else but His All-Holy Will could operate in this way!

Thus the radiation-thrusts or radiations penetrate all Creation, but in such force as they have *never been before.*

Nothing can hide from the effect! And thus, in the Law of the Working of Creation, the Ray of Divine Power also strikes *every soul* at the appointed hour.

When the Divine Ray, which is completely invisible to the human soul, falls upon it, everything that still clings to it must revive and also become manifest, active, *thereby* enabling the last link in the cycle to be closed, either pressing the soul down or raising it up.

Whatever of wrong or evil such a soul in the course of its existence has already been able to throw off, through redemptive experiences according to the Laws of Creation, is obliterated, and in such a way as if it had never been; thus it no longer clings to the soul, it is then no longer imprinted upon it. The soul is freed from it and pure, and therefore can suffer no harm from it.

Only that which has *not* yet come to the closing of its cycle, and therefore still clings to and is connected with the soul, is forthwith driven to the closing of the cycle in the pressure of the Light, in that as it comes to life it *reveals* itself as it attempts to become active, and in so doing also receives the blow it deserves.

The actual blows depend entirely on the strength of the individual volition which, being released in the *reciprocal action,* is directed *against* the soul as the point of origin! Everything, be it good or evil, is now strengthened by the irresistible pressure of the Light and thrust back to the starting-point, to the soul.

And everything which otherwise, in the cumbersome movement of the condensed, hardened environment of all the human souls on earth, might still have required many thousands of years to close the cycle, is now, through the power of the blows from the Light, compressed into a few months in the impetus that is unexpected by mankind.

Such is the manifestation of the World Judgment in its simple naturalness! This time it *is* the *"Last Judgment",* so often proclaimed to you! But its manifestations are entirely different from what you thought. What was formerly proclaimed to you was given *in pictures,* because you would not otherwise have understood it at all.

By means of the Grail Message, however, your knowledge of the working in Creation goes further, and therefore more and more can be revealed to you; for today you are already able to understand it through my Message.

The sword-thrusts of the Judgment-Day strike as strong Light-radiations into Creation, and flow through all the channels that have already been formed through the automatic working of the Divine Laws in Creation, which are based on all the intuitive perceptions, thoughts, volitions and also actions of men as starting-points.

The judging rays are therefore guided with infallible certainty through these existing channels to all souls, and there take effect according to the state of the souls concerned, but in *such* an accelerated way that their whole existence is brought to the *final closing of the cycle* of all past activities within a few months; and in exact accordance with their actual condition these souls will be uplifted or cast down, animated and strengthened or destroyed!

Such is the Judgment! *Today* you are able through the Message to understand the process thus described.

Formerly you could not have grasped it, and therefore everything had to be revealed in simple pictures which correspond more or less to the operation of the process. –

And these blows of the Last Judgment are already on their way to you, to each one in Creation, no matter whether he is with or without his physical body.

The first blows have already reached you, and everything that still clings to your souls is revived.

But also the *final* blows bringing destruction or upliftment have been sent out with an all-overwhelming severity to complete the purification upon this earth! Already they are rushing towards mankind, and nothing can check them anywhere. At the exact hour appointed by God, mankind will be inexorably but justly struck by them! –

THE MILLENNIUM

LIKE a legend it floats in the minds of many people who know of the prophecy, but it is vague, without form, because no one knows how to come to the right conception of it!

The Millennium! Wiseacres have tried again and again to put forward an explanation of how this great period of peace and joy that is implied in it is going to be realised. But it has never yet been possible to come any nearer the truth! They have all gone wrong because they have assigned far too great a role to earthmen, as always happens with everything men think. Moreover, they approved of and built upon existing concepts, and thus every one of these theories had to be regarded as wrong from the start, no matter what its nature.

And then man forgot the principal thing! He did not take into account the condition that was also foretold, that *before* the thousand-year Reign of Peace *everything* has to become *new* in the Judgment! That is the essential foundation for the New Kingdom. It cannot be built up on the existing soil! *Everything* that is old has first to become new!

This does not mean, however, that the old is to be revitalised in its existing form, but the expression "new" implies a change, a transformation of the old!

In his pondering man failed to take this into consideration, and therefore never made any progress towards a right conception.

What must first change most drastically in the Judgment is man himself; for he alone has brought the confusion into Subsequent Creation. From him, from his wrong volition, the evil went forth into the world.

The original beauty, purity and health that always result from a swinging in the Primordial Laws of Creation were gradually distorted and perverted through the wrong volition of this humanity. Instead of a healthy maturing towards perfection, nothing but caricatures could still form in the unceasing process of development!

Just picture to yourselves a potter sitting at his wheel, before him the clay, pliable enough to be moulded to any shape. The wheel, however, is not turned by the potter himself but by a driving-belt, which in turn is kept in motion by the power of an engine.

By a pressure of his fingers the clay is now shaped in continual rotation, carried out by the wheel on which the clay was placed. Now *as* the finger presses *so* the shape develops, either beautiful, plain or ugly.

The spirit of man also works in the same way in this world, in Subsequent Creation. Through his volition he exercises leadership, thus as spirit he exerts pressure upon certain animistic substance, which shapes both ethereal and gross matter. For a spirit, animistic substance is the finger that exercises the pressure according to the spirit's volition. The clay is ethereal and gross matter; but the movement, which is independent of the human spirit, comprises the automatic movements of the Primordial Laws of Creation, which like currents ceaselessly drive towards the development of everything man forms in his volition.

Thus the volition of the human spirit is answerable for much that develops in Subsequent Creation; for *man* as spirit exercises the pressure that determines the nature of the form. He cannot exercise his will without simultaneously forming! No matter what it is! Thus he can likewise never evade this responsibility for all the forms created by him. His volition, his thinking and his actions – everything takes on form in the mechanism of this world. That man has neither known it, nor wanted to know it, is his concern, is his fault. His ignorance does not alter the effect.

Thus through his wrong volition, his obstinacy and self-conceit, he has not only held back any true blossoming, but has ruined Subsequent Creation and brought about only harm instead of blessing!

Admonitions through prophets, then through the Son of God Himself, were not enough to change man and induce him to take the right course! He did not *want* to, and increasingly nourished his conceited idea of being a world-ruler, in which already lay hidden the germ for his inevitable downfall. This germ grew with his conceit, and prepared the catastrophes that must now be unleashed according to the Eternal Law in Creation, which man failed to recognise because his conceited idea of being the master prevented him from doing so.

The sole cause of the coming horrors lies in the distortion of the Divine Primordial Laws through the false volition of these human spirits in Subse-

174

quent Creation! For this wrong volition threw into confusion all the power-currents that take effect automatically. The diversion of their course, however, cannot go unpunished since, knotted and entangled as they are, they will then *forcibly* detach themselves at a certain time. The detaching and disentangling shows itself in the manifestations that we call catastrophes. It makes no difference whether this occurs in public affairs, in families, with individuals or entire peoples, or with the forces of nature.

Thereby all that is false will collapse, judging itself through the power that is in these currents, which have been wrongly directed by humanity's conceit, contrary to what God willed; for these currents can *only* bring about blessing when they follow *those* courses which are intended for them by Primordial Law, thus ordained for them by the Creator. Never otherwise.

That is also why the end could be foreseen already thousands of years ago, because owing to the wrongly-willed attitude of men it could not possibly come about any differently, since the final result of anything that happens always remains strictly bound to the Primordial Laws.

Now since the human spirits have proved their utter inability to recognise their task in this Creation, since they proved their unwillingness to fulfil it by repudiating and misinterpreting all the warnings given by called ones and prophets, even those by the Son of God Himself, sealing their enmity by the crucifixion, God now *forcibly* intervenes.

Hence the Millennium!

Only by *force* can Subsequent Creation still be helped, as well as mankind, who have proved that they would never voluntarily be persuaded to take the right path which they must follow in Creation in order to live in it according to God's Will, and also to work and bring blessing as *the* beings that they really are by virtue of their spiritual nature.

For this reason mankind now, in the Judgment, are being *deprived of their rights,* they are for a time *disinherited* of the right they have possessed up till now, the right that the *human will* rules over this Subsequent Creation, guiding and forming it! Disinherited for a thousand years, so that at last there may be peace, and a striving towards the Light in accordance with the Primordial Laws in Creation, to which man has hitherto been hostile.

Disinheriting humanity of all the rights hitherto held in Subsequent Creation therefore makes possible and safeguards the establishment of the long-wished-for Kingdom of Peace! *Thus* does man stand before his God! *For that* must he now render account. *That* is the meaning of and the necessity for the thousand-year Kingdom of God here on earth. A sad truth, which cannot be more shaming for this mankind! But ... it is the only way to help them.

Thus the Millennium will become *a school for mankind,* in which they must learn *how* they have to stand in this Subsequent Creation, how to think and to act in order to fulfil their appointed task correctly, and thereby to achieve happiness themselves!

To this end the will of mankind as ruler in Subsequent Creation is now suspended for a thousand years, after whatever he has wrongly sown and wrongly guided has been destroyed in the Judgment!

During the thousand years the Will of God alone will reign supreme, to Which every human spirit must submit as soon as he has been able to pass through the Judgment!

But should there be another failure as in the past, then mankind must count on complete annihilation!

Such is the Millennium and its purpose! In their self-conceit and the delusion of their own importance, mankind have imagined it to be quite different. But they will have to learn and experience it as it actually is!

Therein also lies only a *Grace* of God, to help those who are really of a pure volition!

A NECESSARY WORD

BE ON your guard, spirit of man, for your hour has come! The time which you so ardently desired, which is granted to you for your development – you have spent it only in wickedness!

Beware, in your presumptuous intellectual conceit that has thrown you into the arms of Darkness, which today holds you triumphantly in its clutches!

Look upwards! You are standing in the Divine Judgment!

Awake and tremble, you who in your narrow-mindedness and limited outlook swarm around the golden calf of earthly transience, like moths attracted by a deceptive brightness. It was because of you that Moses, in his wrath of disappointment, once shattered those tablets of the Laws of your God that were to help you to ascend to the Light.

This breaking of the tablets was the living symbol that the entire humanity did not deserve to have knowledge of this Will of God, of the Will Which they rejected in their wanton behaviour and earthly arrogance, in order to dance round a self-made idol and thereby follow their own desires!

Now, however, the end is at hand in the final reaction, in the consequences, in the retribution! For now *you* will be shattered by the Will once so frivolously rejected!

Neither lamentations nor pleading will help any more; for you were given thousands of years to come to your senses! But you never had time for that! You did not want to, and even today, with incorrigible arrogance, you think yourselves much too wise. That *just in this* the greatest stupidity reveals itself, you do not want to see. Thereby you have finally become troublesome vermin in this world, no longer knowing anything other than wilfully to revile all Light, because with your persistence in grubbing about only in the Darkness you have lost every possibility of seeking with a free upward gaze, of recognising or of being able to bear Light.

Thus you are now branded by yourselves!

Therefore as soon as the Light once more shines forth you will stagger back dazzled, and beyond help sink into the abyss that has even now opened up behind you, waiting to engulf those who have thus been rejected!

There you shall be bound in an inescapable grip, so that all those who strive to aspire to the Light may find the way thereto in blissful recognition, free from your presumption and your hankering to accept tinsel instead of pure gold! Sink into that death-dealing horror, which you have prepared for yourselves with the most stubborn efforts! In future you shall no longer be able to obscure the Divine Truth!

How zealously they try, these little human beings, to push their ridiculous pseudo-knowledge well into the foreground, and how do they thereby confuse so many souls who could be saved if they did not fall into the hands of spiritual highwaymen, who like brigands still prowl about the first stretch of the right path, *apparently* following the same road. But what is it that they really offer? With great pompousness and hackneyed phrases they proudly take their stand on traditions, the true meaning of which they have never understood.

Very apt is the popular saying about this: they are threshing empty straw! Empty because they have not also picked up the real kernels, for which they lack understanding. One comes up against such narrow-mindedness everywhere; with dull obstinacy they ride upon the phrases of others, because they themselves have nothing to contribute.

There are thousands of these, and again thousands who imagine that they *alone* possess the true faith! Wherever they meet with anything beyond their comprehension they humbly, and with inner satisfaction, warn against arrogance! *These belong among the worst!* They are the very ones who are even now rejected, because their religious obduracy makes it impossible ever to help them. Once they realise their error no dread, no lamenting and no petitioning will be of any avail. They did not want it otherwise, they missed their opportunity. There shall be no mourning over them. Each moment is far too precious still to be wasted on those who think they know everything better; for they will never in any case come to an awakening from their obstinacy, but will blindly perish in it! With nauseating words and assurances of their faith in God, their purely imaginary recognition of Christ!

In no better case are the masses of those who attend their Divine Services with the regularity and duty they apply to other work; because it is necessary

178

and advantageous, expedient. Partly also out of habit or because it is the "custom". Perhaps also out of simple prudence because, after all, "one never knows to what good it might ultimately lead". *Like a breath in the wind they will vanish!* –

More to be pitied are those investigators who with their really earnest inquiring mind fail still to rise from the brushwood in which they tirelessly rummage, expecting to discover *in it* a way to the beginning of Creation. Nevertheless it is all useless, and there is no excuse for it! Besides there are only a few, a very few. Most of those who call themselves investigators become lost in meaningless trifling.

The great remainder of mankind, however, *have no time* for "introspection". Apparently they are very harassed human beings, burdened with quite enough work in order to achieve fulfilment of their earthly desires, their daily needs, but ultimately also of things going far beyond that. They do not notice that with the fulfilment their wishes also increase, whereby a final aim never comes in sight, and thus the striving one can *never* find the peace or the time for *inner* awakening! Without any high goal for eternity, he allows himself to be hurried through his earth-life, enslaved to his earthly desires.

Exhausted by such activities, he must finally also care for his body through rest, change and diversion. So of course he has no time left for anything beyond the earthly, for the spiritual! But should his intuitive perception occasionally and very softly make itself felt with the thought of what comes "after death", then at best he becomes somewhat pensive for a few moments, but never allows himself to be stirred and awakened by it; instead, he then brusquely and quickly represses all such things, complaining that he cannot occupy himself with them even if he really wanted to! He simply has not *any* time for it!

Many a one would even like to see *others* creating the opportunity for it. Quite often there are also accusations against fate and murmurings against God! Naturally every word is wasted on such as these, because they are *never willing* to acknowledge that it depended solely upon themselves to shape their lives differently!

For them there are only *earthly* needs, which always increase with every success. They have never *seriously* wished for anything else. They have always raised all kinds of obstacles against it. They have frivolously relegated it to the fifth or sixth place, only to be thought of in dire need or at the approach of death. Until now it has remained a matter of secondary importance for all ... who have time!

And if one day there presented itself, *plainly recognisable, the opportunity* to concern oneself seriously with it, then immediately new and special wishes, which are really nothing more than excuses, would arise, such as: "But *first* I still want to do this and that, then I am quite prepared to study it." Exactly as Christ once said!

Nowhere is there to be found that seriousness which is absolutely imperative for this most essential of all matters! It seemed to them too remote. For this reason they are now *all* rejected, all of them! Not one of them will be admitted into the Kingdom of God!

Rotten fruit for ascent, who only spread further decay around them. Now reflect for yourselves, who *then* can still remain! A sad picture! But unfortunately only too true. –

And when now the Judgment causes mankind to yield they will very quickly kneel in the dust! But just envisage already *today how* they will kneel: In all wretchedness, but at the same time once more arrogantly; for again they will only be lamenting and *begging that help may be given to them!*

The heavy burden which they have imposed on themselves, and which finally threatens to crush them, *should be taken from them! That* then is what they petition for! Do you hear it? Their petitions are for alleviation of their torment, but without at the same time one thought for their own inner improvement! Not *one* honest wish for voluntary alteration of their hitherto wrong thinking, of their purely earthly pursuits! Not *one* wish to recognise and bravely acknowledge their present errors and faults.

And then, when the Son of Man comes among them in the great affliction, no doubt all their hands will be stretched out to Him, with whining and beseeching, yet again only in the hope that He will *help them in the way they wish,* thus ending their suffering and leading them to new life!

But He will push away the majority of these petitioners like poisonous vermin! For after receiving help, all such imploring ones would immediately relapse into their old faults, poisoning their environment at the same time. He will accept *only* those who plead to Him for strength finally to pull themselves together for permanent improvement, who humbly strive to throw off all former stubbornness, and joyfully greet the Word of Truth from the Light as redemption! –

180

But an understanding of the Grail Message, as well as of the previous Message of the Son of God, will only become possible when a human spirit casts aside *everything* that it has built up with its imagined understanding, *and starts from the very beginning!* In this they must first become like children! A leading across from the present errors is impossible. From the ground up there must be a complete *newness,* which grows and becomes strong out of simplicity and humility.

If mankind were helped in the way they ask in the hour of danger and need, then everything would once more be quickly forgotten as soon as their terror was removed. With their lack of understanding they would again unscrupulously begin to criticise instead of to reflect.

Such a waste of time is quite impossible in the future, since the existence of this part of the world has to hasten towards its end. Henceforth for every human spirit it is: Either – Or! Salvation from self-created entanglements or destruction therein!

The choice is free. But the consequences of the decision are definite and irrevocable!

As though released from a great pressure, those saved will then breathe freely and exult after the repulsive, unclean Darkness, with the creatures that gladly cling to it, has at last had to go down where it belongs, through the sword-thrusts of the Light!

Then the earth, purified of all pestilential thoughts, will arise like a virgin, and peace will blossom for all mankind!

FOR YEARS now "knowing ones" have been speaking of the coming of this especially significant Star. The number of those who await it is continually increasing, and the indications become more and more definite, so much so that in fact it is to be expected soon. But *what* it really signifies, what it brings, whence it comes, has not yet been rightly explained.

It is thought that it brings upheavals of an incisive nature. But this Star portends more.

It *can* be called the Star of Bethlehem, because it is of exactly the same nature as that was. Its power sucks the waters up high, brings weather catastrophes and still more. When encircled by its rays the earth quakes.

Since the event in Bethlehem there has been nothing like it. Like the Star of Bethlehem, this Star has also detached itself from the Eternal Realm of Primordial Spirit at such a time as to take effect on this earth exactly when the years of spiritual enlightenment are to come to all mankind.

The Star takes its course in a *straight* line from the Eternal Realm to this part of the Universe. Its core is filled with high spiritual power; it envelops itself in material substance, and will thereby also become visible to men on earth. Unerringly and unswervingly the Comet pursues its course, and will appear on the scene at the right hour, as already ordained thousands of years ago.

The first direct effects have already begun in recent years. For anyone who wishes neither to see nor to hear this, and who does not perceive how ridiculous it is still to maintain that all the *extraordinary* things which have already happened are of everyday occurrence, there is naturally no help. He either wishes to act like an ostrich out of fear, or he is burdened with an extremely limited understanding. Both types must be allowed to go serenely on their way; one can only smile at their easily refutable assertions.

But the knowing ones could also be told where the first *powerful* rays are striking. However, since the rays are gradually also encompassing the whole earth, there is no use in being more explicit. It will take years to come to this point, and years before the Comet again releases the earth from its influence.

And *then* the earth is *purified* and *refreshed* in *every respect* for the blessing and joy of its inhabitants. It will be more beautiful than it has ever been. Therefore every believer shall look forward to the future with tranquil confidence, and not be alarmed at anything that may happen in the coming years. If he can look up with confidence to God no harm will come to him. – –

HE IS called World Teacher not because He is to teach the World, and will perhaps found a religion that unites the World, or more specifically the earth, or better still humanity on earth, or that holds sway over the earth; but He is called World Teacher because He *explains* the "World" and brings the teaching about the World. That which man really must know! He teaches how to *recognise* the "World" in its automatic activity, so that earthman may adjust himself accordingly, and thereby be able consciously to ascend in the recognition of the actual Laws of the World!

Thus it is really a question of cosmology, of instruction about the World, about Creation.

Behind this *true* World Teacher, visible to *pure clairvoyants,* stands radiantly the great *Cross of Redemption,* as once it did with Christ! It can also be said: *"He bears the Cross"!* But that has nothing to do with suffering and martyrdom.

This will be one of the signs which, "living and radiating", no sorcerer or magician however accomplished is able to simulate, and by which the absolute genuineness of His Mission can be recognised!

This "beyond-earthly" happening is not disconnected, not merely arbitrary, therefore not unnatural. The connection will immediately be understood as soon as the true significance of the actual "Cross of Redemption" is known. The Cross of Redemption does not have the same meaning as Christ's Cross of Suffering, through which indeed mankind could not be redeemed, as I explain in detail in the lecture "The Crucifixion of the Son of God and the Lord's Supper", and repeat many times. It is something quite different, again of apparent simplicity, yet of immense greatness!

The Cross was already known before Christ's time on earth. It is the sign of Divine Truth! Not merely the sign, but the living form for It. And since Christ was the Bringer of Divine Truth, of the genuine One, and came from the Truth, was in direct connection with It, bearing a part of It within Himself, It also clung to Him inwardly and outwardly in a living form! It is *visible* in the living, thus shining and independently *radiating* Cross! It may be said that It is the Cross itself. Where this Radiant Cross is, there also is Truth, since this Cross cannot be separated from Truth; rather they are both one, *because this Cross displays the visible form of Truth.*

The Cross of Rays or the radiating Cross *is* therefore the Truth in its original form. And since man can ascend only through the Truth, and in no other way, the human spirit finds true *redemption* only in the recognition or knowledge of Divine Truth!

Again, since redemption lies only in the Truth, it follows that the Cross, that is, the Truth, is the redeeming Cross, or the *Cross of Redemption!*

It is the Cross of the Redeemer! *The Redeemer, however, is the Truth* for mankind! Only knowledge of the Truth and, connected therewith, making use of the way that lies or is shown in the Truth, can lead the human spirit out of its present derangement and error upwards to the Light, can liberate and redeem it from its present state. And as the Son of God Who was sent, and the Son of Man now coming, are the *sole* Bringers of the *undimmed* Truth, bearing It within Themselves, They must both naturally also bear inseparably the Cross within Themselves, that is, They must be Bearers of the Cross of Rays, Bearers of Truth, Bearers of Redemption, which for humanity lies in the Truth. They bring redemption in the Truth to those who receive It, who thus walk on the path shown. – What is all the clever talk of men beside this? It will fade away in the hour of need.

For that reason the Son of God told men that they should take up the Cross and follow Him, which means *to accept the Truth and to live accordingly!* To adapt themselves to the Laws of Creation, to learn to understand them fully and make only the best use of their automatic effects.

But what has the restricted mind of man once more made of this simple and natural fact! A doctrine of suffering desired neither by God nor the Son of God! And thereby they have taken a *wrong* path, that is not in accord with the path indicated, but leads far away from the Will of God, Which desires only to lead to joy instead of suffering.

It is naturally a terrible symbol for mankind that at that time the Son of God was nailed by them just to the earthly representation of the form of Truth, and tortured to death, thus going to His earthly destruction on the symbol of the Truth which He brought! The Cross of Suffering of the churches, however, is *not* the Cross of Redemption!

185

It is said of the Son of God: "He who stands in the Power and the Truth". The Power is the Will of God, the Holy Spirit. Its visible form is the Dove. The visible form of Truth is the independently radiating Cross. Both were seen – living – with the Son of God, because He stood in them. Thus with Him it was a natural and self-evident manifestation.

The same will also be seen with the Son of Man! The Dove above Him, the Cross of Redemption behind Him; for He again is inseparably linked with them as the Bringer of Truth, "Who stands in the Power and the Truth"! *They are the infallible signs of His genuine Mission to fulfil the prophecies.* The signs that can never be imitated, which are indestructible, warning, and despite the fearfulness of the severity also promising! Before these alone must the Darkness yield!

Look upwards! As soon as the inexorable harbingers of His coming have appeared, clearing the way for Him of the obstacles that human conceit heaps upon it, *the bandage will fall from the eyes of many* to whom is granted the grace to recognise Him *thus!* Then, forced by the power of the Light, they will *have* to bear witness openly.

Not one of the false prophets and of the leaders, today still so numerous, is able to stand his ground against *this;* for in these two sublime signs, which no one but the Son of God and the Son of Man can bear, God Himself speaks for His Servant, and all human wisdom must become silent because of them. – Watch for that hour, it will be nearer than *all* men think.

THE STRANGER

ONCE more Darkness had settled over the earth. Triumphantly it over-shadowed men, and barred their way to the Primordial Spiritual Realm. The Light of God had withdrawn from them. The body that had served It as an earthly vessel hung bleeding and mutilated on the Cross, as a victim of the protest of those to whom It wished to bring happiness and holy peace.

At the summit of the entire Creation, in the radiant vicinity of God, stands the Grail Castle as the Temple of Light. Deep grief prevailed there over the erring human spirits far below who, blindly imagining that they knew every-thing better, closed themselves in hostility to the Truth, and allowed them-selves to be driven so far by the hate-filled Darkness as to commit this crime against the Son of God. The curse thus created by mankind fell heavily on the whole world, pressing them into an even greater limitation of under-standing. –

Gravely perplexed, a youth beheld this monstrous happening from the Castle of the Grail ... the future Son of Man. He was then already being pre-pared for His Mission, a process which took thousands of years; for He was to descend well-equipped into those lower regions where, through the vol-ition of mankind, Darkness reigned.

A woman's hand was gently laid on the shoulder of the dreaming one. The Queen of Womanhood stood beside Him, and spoke in a sad and loving voice:

"Let this event impress itself upon you, dear son. *Such* is the battlefield through which you will have to pass in the hour of fulfilment; for at the re-quest of the murdered Saviour God the Father grants that before the Judg-ment you shall once more proclaim His Word to the faithless, in order to save those who are still willing to listen to It!"

The youth bowed His head in silence and sent up a fervent prayer for strength, for such great Divine Love re-echoed mightily within Him!

The tidings of the last, of another possibility of Grace spread rapidly through all the spheres, and many souls besought God to grant that they might be permitted to help in the great work of the redemption of all those who still wish to find the way to God. The Love of God the Father granted this to many a soul, who was thereby helped in its ascent. In grateful joy the host of these so blessed ones jubilantly gave a solemn pledge of loyalty to fulfil the opportunity of serving that was granted them.

Thus *those* Called ones were trained, who were later to hold themselves at the disposal of the Envoy of God when His hour of fulfilment on earth came. They were carefully developed for these tasks and incarnated on earth at the right time, so that they might be ready whenever the Call reached them, *and their first fulfilment of duty remained to listen for this Call!*

Meanwhile the legacy of the murdered Son of God, His Living Word, was exploited on earth solely for selfish purposes. Mankind had no conception of the true Principles of Christ. On the contrary, they gradually grew into such a wrong and purely earthly doctrine of love that finally they rejected anything else as not coming from God, and they still today reject and revile whatever does not conform to this nauseating sentimentality desired by them, and what does not practise a similar and very unwholesome servile worship of mankind.

Everything that does not have as its foundation the acknowledgment of the supremacy of man is simply labelled as false, and not belonging to the Word of God. This behaviour, however, actually only conceals the uneasy apprehension that the long-felt hollowness of the false edifice might become apparent.

This is what had been made of the sacred legacy of the Son of God! On such degrading assumptions His clear words were interpreted and passed on in all too human a way. Adherents were solicited through courting human frailties, until some earthly power could be developed, which has always remained the ultimate goal. Then, however, by their brutal cruelties they very soon showed how far the bearers of the misconstrued Christ-Principle were from the real understanding of it, and how little they lived it.

Continually and ever more clearly there was proof that the very ones who wished to be the bearers of the Christ-Principle were shamelessly and unpardonably the worst enemies and greatest offenders against the true Christ-Principle! After Christ's life on earth the whole of history, from the beginning of the churches, sets forth these facts so clearly, in letters so indelibly engraved and branded, that they can never be denied or glossed over. The stigma of conscious hypocrisy was undisguisably established throughout the long history of individual and mass murders under unpardonable invocations of God, and even today this is being extended in many places, but in different forms adapted to the present time.

Thus, thanks to the willingness of all the human spirits, the Darkness became ever denser as the time approached when the Son of Man had to be incarnated upon earth.

Joyful activity in the elements heralded the earthly birth. Angels lovingly accompanied Him down to this earth. Primordial Beings formed a solid rampart around Him and around His earthly childhood. His earthly youth was allowed to be bright and sunny. In the evenings He saw the Comet, radiant above Him, like a greeting from God the Father; He regarded it as nothing unusual, as one of the other stars, until the bandage which He had to wear during His bitter training on earth was put before His eyes.

Then life around Him seemed strange; only a great unquenchable longing filled His soul, increasing to a restlessness, to a continual nervous seeking. Nothing the earth offered could satisfy it.

With the ethereal bandage over His eyes, He now stood on hostile ground facing the Darkness, on a battlefield where everything dark could have a firmer foothold than He Himself. Therefore it was only natural that wherever He sought to undertake something He could find no response and no success, but only the Darkness hissed up in enmity every time.

As long as the time of fulfilment for Him had not arrived, the Darkness could always remain stronger, and could inflict material damage upon Him wherever He engaged in some earthly affairs; for everything earthly quite naturally *had* to oppose the Envoy of God with nothing but hostility, because all human volition today is directed *against* the true Will of God in spite of the alleged search for Truth, behind which there always lurks only self-conceit in various forms. The Darkness easily found willing creatures everywhere to hinder the Envoy from the Light, and to injure Him grievously and painfully.

Thus His time of learning on earth became the path of suffering.

Just as spiritual substance, with great power, appears to have a magnetically attracting and holding effect upon animistic, ethereal and gross material substances, so in a similar and much more powerful way whatever has its origin above the spiritual in Subsequent Creation must exert an influence on *everything* that lies below it. This is perfectly natural, it could not be otherwise. However, it only resembles the power of attraction in its manifestation. The power of attraction in the ordinary sense is effective only among homogeneous species.

But *here* it is a question of the existing *power of the stronger* in a purely objective and most noble sense! It is not to be thought of in an earthly human way; for in the World of Gross Matter this Law, like everything else, has been coarsened in its effect through the actions of men. The natural effect of this dominant power reveals itself outwardly like a magnet attracting, uniting, holding together and controlling.

Now because of this Law, men too felt themselves magnetically drawn to this veiled, more powerful Stranger from On High, although often resisting Him with enmity. The thick veils He wore around Him could not entirely prevent the emanation of this power that was alien on earth; while on the other hand this power could not yet radiate freely either to exert *that* irresistible might which it has after the falling away of the covering veils in the hour of fulfilment.

This brought conflict among the intuitive perceptions of men. The very being of the Stranger was enough to awaken in those who met Him hopes of the most varied kinds which alas, because of their attitude, were always brought down to merely earthly wishes, which they nourished and fostered within themselves.

The Stranger, however, could never heed such wishes, since His hour had not yet come. Thereby many were often greatly disappointed through their own imaginings and, strange to say, even felt themselves deceived. They never reflected that in reality it was *only their own* selfish expectations which were not fulfilled and, indignant about this through their disappointment, they laid the responsibility for it on the Stranger. Yet He did not call them; but they forced themselves upon and clung to Him because of this Law which was unknown to them, and they often became a heavy burden to Him, with which He journeyed through *those* years on earth that were ordained for Him as His time of learning.

Men on earth perceived something mysterious and unknown about Him, which they could not explain, they sensed a hidden might which they did not understand, and in the end through their ignorance they naturally suspected only intentional suggestion, hypnotism and magic, according to the nature of their lack of understanding; whereas there was no question of any of these. Their original attachment, the consciousness of being strangely attracted, then very often turned into hatred, which expressed itself in moral stone-throwing and attempts to defile Him from Whom they had expected much – too soon.

No one took the trouble to make a just self-examination, which would have revealed that the Stranger, living apart with different views and ideals, was the one made use of by those who crowded towards Him, but not that He had taken advantage of anyone, as the obtruders, in their bitterness over the non-fulfilment of their desires for a life of ease, encouraged themselves and others to believe. Blindly they repaid the friendliness shown them with senseless hate and enmity, similar to the deed of Judas.

But the Stranger on earth had to bear everything patiently; for it was only a quite natural consequence of His existence, so long as mankind were still living in error. By this alone He, to Whom all wrong-doing and wrong thinking were entirely alien, was able to recognise what earthmen in their nature could become capable of. At the same time, however, such experiences also gave Him the necessary hardening, which slowly laid itself like an armour around His otherwise ever-present helpfulness, and thus created a gulf between that and mankind ... through the wounds inflicted upon His soul, which brought about a separation, and which can only be healed through the complete change in mankind. These wounds inflicted on Him have formed from that hour the gulf which can be bridged only by *that* man *who wholly* follows the road of the Laws of God. This alone can serve as a bridge. Everyone else must be dashed to pieces in the abyss; for there is no other way over it. And to remain standing before it means destruction.

At the exact hour, even before the end of this arduous time of learning, the meeting came to pass with *that* Companion Who as a Part of Him was to journey with Him through earthly life, to participate in the great task according to Divine Ordinance. Herself a Stranger on earth, She joyfully entered the Will of God through Her own recognition, and gratefully merged with It.

Only then came the time for the Called ones, who had once solemnly pledged to God their loyalty for service! The granting of their petition had been carefully carried out. At the appropriate time they were incarnated on earth. Through faithful guidance they were equipped in the earthly sense with everything they needed for the fulfilment of their respective tasks. It was brought, given to them, so noticeably that they simply could not consider it other than as a gift, as a loan for the hour of fulfilment of their former promise.

At the precise moment they came into contact with the Envoy, through His Word, and then also personally ... but many of them, although they sensed the Call and intuitively perceived something unusual in their souls, had meanwhile in the course of their earth-life permitted themselves to be so ensnared by purely earthly matters, and to some extent even by the Darkness, that they could not summon up the strength to conquer themselves for the true service, to fulfil which they were permitted to come to earth for this great time.

A few did show a faint willingness to fulfil, yet their earthly faults held them back from it. Unfortunately there were also others who certainly set out on the path of their mission, but who from the very beginning sought *first* of all to gain earthly advantage for themselves thereby. Even among those of earnest volition there were several who expected Him Whom *they* had to serve to smooth their way to the fulfilment, instead of the reverse.

Only a few isolated ones really showed themselves capable of growing into their task. To these was then given in the hour of fulfilment ten times greater strength, so that the gaps were no longer perceptible, and in loyalty they became capable of accomplishing even more than the great throng could ever have achieved. –

It was with grief that the Stranger on earth saw the havoc among the group of the Called ones. *That was one of the most bitter experiences for Him!* Much as He had learned, much as He suffered at the hands of men ... before this last fact He stood uncomprehending; for He found no excuse whatever for this failure. In His conception a Called one who, in the granting of his petition, was specially guided and incarnated, could do no other than faithfully carry out his task in the most joyous fulfilment! For what other purpose was he on earth! Why had he been faithfully guarded up to the hour when the Envoy needed him! Everything had been given to him solely for the sake of his necessary service.

So it was that the Stranger, on meeting the first Called ones, put His full trust in them. He regarded them only as friends, who simply could not think,

192

intuitively perceive and act in any other way than in the most steadfast loyal-ty. Was it not the highest, the most precious privilege that could fall to the lot of a human being. The possibility never entered His mind that even Called ones could have become impure during their time of waiting. It was incon-ceivable to Him that any human being, in view of such grace, could wantonly neglect and trifle away the real purpose of his earth-life. With the faults cling-ing to them they only appeared to Him as being in need of great help ... And so the dreadfulness of a recognition struck Him all the more severely when He had to experience that even in such exceptional cases the human spirit is not reliable, and that it shows itself unworthy of the highest blessing even with the most faithful spiritual guidance!

Deeply shaken, He suddenly saw before Him mankind in all their un-speakable inferiority and depravity. They filled Him with disgust.

Misery fell more oppressively upon the earth. The instability of the false structure of all that mankind had hitherto produced became ever more appar-ent. Proof of their incapacity came more plainly to light. With the increasing confusion everything slowly began to sway, with one exception: Man's con-ceit in his own imagined abilities.

This was just what sprang up more luxuriantly than ever, which was quite natural, because conceit always needs the soil of narrow-mindedness. The in-crease of narrow-mindedness must also bring with it an abundant growth of conceit.

The craving for importance increased to a feverish frenzy. The less man had to offer the more his soul, which forebodingly sensed only too well that it was sinking, cried out anxiously within him for liberation, the more he then, in his false desire to keep his balance, obtrusively pursued *outward earthly trif-les* and human honours. Even if in quiet moments men at last began to doubt themselves, this only made them the more eager to have at least a *reputation* for knowledge. At *all* costs!

Thus things went rapidly downhill. In the fear-producing recognition of the approaching collapse, each in his own way finally thought to dull him-self, letting the outrageous state of affairs continue to take its course. He closed his eyes to the menacing responsibility.

"Wise" men, however, proclaimed the time of the coming of a strong helper out of the distress. But most of them wanted to see this helper in themselves or, if they were modest, at least to find him within their circle.

The "faithful" prayed to God for help out of the confusion. But it became evident that these petty earthmen, even while praying in expectation of a fulfilment, sought inwardly to impose conditions upon God by wishing for *such* a helper as would correspond with *their views*. So far-reaching are the results of earthly narrow-mindedness. Mankind can believe that an Envoy of God needs to adorn Himself with earthly honours! They expect Him to adapt Himself to their narrow-minded earthly opinions in order to be acknowledged by them, and *thereby* to win their faith and confidence. What incredible conceit, what arrogance, lie in this fact alone! In the hour of fulfilment the conceit will be completely shattered, along with all those who inwardly indulged in such a delusion! –

Then the Lord called to His Servant, Who was walking the earth as a Stranger, that He should speak and give tidings to all those who were thirsting for it!

And behold, the knowledge of the "wise ones" was false, the prayers of the faithful were not genuine; for they did not open themselves to the Voice that came forth from the Truth, and which therefore could only be recognised where the spark of Truth within man had not been buried by earthly wrongdoing, the domination of the intellect, and all those things that tend to crowd the human spirit from the right path and cause its downfall.

It could only awaken an echo where the petition came from a truly humble and honest soul.

The Call went forth! Wherever it struck it brought disquiet and dissension. But in those places where it was earnestly awaited it brought peace and happiness.

The Darkness began to stir restlessly, and massed ever more densely, heavily and gloomily around the earth. Here and there it was already hissing up malignantly, and spitting in hate into the ranks of those who wished to obey the Call. Ever more closely it surrounded *those* Called ones who, through their failure, were forced to sink away into the Darkness, to which they had thereby voluntarily held out their hand. Their former solemn vow bound them fast to the Envoy spiritually, and drew them to Him at the hour of the approaching fulfilment, while their faults formed obstacles and repelled them from Him, because a connection with the Light was thus impossible.

Now from this there could in turn only arise a bridge for hate, for the whole hate of the Darkness against all that is Light. And so they intensified the path of suffering of the Envoy from the Light until it became a Golgotha, and the majority of mankind only too gladly joined in making it more difficult; especially those who imagined that they already knew and were following the path of the Light themselves, as once the Pharisees and Scribes did.

All this created a situation in which mankind could prove once more that they would again behave in exactly the same way today as long ago they acted against the Son of God. Only this time in a more modern form, a symbolic crucifixion through an attempt at *moral murder,* which according to the Laws of God *is no less punishable than physical murder.*

It was fulfilment after the last opportunity of mercy had been frivolously neglected. Traitors, false witnesses and slanderers came from the ranks of those who had been called. Base minions of the Darkness ventured to approach in ever increasing numbers, since they felt themselves secure, because in fulfilment the Stranger on earth kept silent when confronted with this filth, as He had been commanded to do, and as once the Son of God also was silent before the howling mob that wanted to have Him nailed to the cross as a criminal.

But when the faithless deserters in their blind hate already thought themselves close to victory, and the Darkness once more assumed that the Work of the Light had been destroyed, because it hoped that the Bearer of this Work had been rendered quite impotent on earth, then this time God revealed *His Will with Omnipotence!* And then ... even the mockers sank trembling to their knees, but ... for them it was too late!

SALVATION! REDEMPTION!

SALVATION! Redemption! How often already have human beings pictured these words wrongly to themselves, when they wanted to see in them unconditional help from the Light, to the exclusion of the All-Holy Justice! This implies a total error, that is already evident today in everything devised by the human mind. They want to make God into their helpful slave, who is only to be considered in connection with the welfare of insignificant earthmen.

Just ask yourselves for once about this, throw light on your thoughts without extenuation, delve into them clearly and objectively, then you will have to confess that your whole thinking has never been attuned other than to the idea that, upon your petitions, God should always serve and help you to fulfil your wishes.

Of course you do not speak of it in terms that would be more according to the nature of your being, but as always give another name to your false volition, putting on little cloaks of deceptive humility, and only speaking of "granting" instead of serving; yet this does not alter the fact that your whole conduct, even when praying, is dominated by evil and cannot be pleasing to God!

At last be honest with yourselves for once, and tremble at the recognition of how you have hitherto always stood before your God, stubborn, arrogant and discontented, hypocritical because of your superficiality, thinking of Him only in misery and distress so that He may help you out of the consequences of your actions; but you have never asked beforehand whether your decisions really were according to *His* Will.

What are you men before the Omnipotence and Sublimity of the Lord, Whom you would have rule over you just *as* it pleases you! With what presumption you would like to enforce here on earth *those* laws that come from your narrow way of thinking, and that are not in harmony with the Divine Laws that He placed in Creation. You so often exercise your wrong volition, with a cunning and evil-mindedness that is inexcusable before God, harming your neighbours thereby to gain advantages for yourselves, either in money or goods, or to acquire a reputation with those for whom you do it.

All this will now fall heavily upon you with the weight of a mountain; for nothing of all your wrong-doing could be cancelled in the Law of Reciprocal Action as having been redeemed, unless you freed yourselves through the change in your volition for what is good.

The barriers that still hold back the collapse of the piled-up mass of reprisals are torn away! Everything rolls down irresistibly on earthly humanity, who would like to continue in spiritual indolence and arrogance in order to enforce their will, which has long since strayed far from the Will of God.

This, however, is the end for the dominion of all Darkness on earth! It will collapse, and drag down all those human beings who have sided with it.

But in the midst of the thundering roar of the collapse, the Word rings out! Victoriously It resounds through the lands, so that those who honestly *strive* for It may still save themselves.

The condition implied is that each one must himself strive to recognise the Word of the Lord as salvation! If he doubts and allows this last opportunity to pass without making use of it with all his strength, he will never again be in this position, and the moment for him to find redemption is forever lost.

Salvation, redemption, will only come to him in the Word, Which he must absorb, so that by living in accordance with It he may release himself from the bonds that hold him down through misunderstanding and distorting the true concepts.

You have been most seriously poisoned and endangered by the false representation of the Love of God, which you sought to divest of all vigour, all power and clarity, enveloping it instead in an unhealthy weakness and harmful indulgence, which was bound to plunge you all together into spiritual indolence and thus into ruin.

Beware of the fatal distortion of the concept of the Holy Love of God! You therewith fall into a slumber which at first is pleasant, but which becomes the sleep of death.

True love does not lie in indulgence, and in a kindness that is expected to forgive everything. This is wrong, and acts like a drug that only lulls the spirits into lassitude and weakness, finally bringing on complete paralysis and enforcing eternal death, since an awakening at the right time is then impossible.

Only the severe coolness of Divine Purity can penetrate the lassitude, and pave the way for the true Love that leads to your spirits. Purity *is* severe, It knows neither extenuation nor excuse. Therefore It will probably appear ruthless to many a person who only too willingly tries to deceive himself. But actually It only hurts where something is not in order.

Weakness brings harm to yourselves as well as to those whom you imagine you are pleasing by it. In time you will be judged by a *Higher One* with the kind of justice that has become strange to you for a long time through yourselves, for you have withdrawn from it.

It is the *Divine Justice,* unchangeable from eternity to eternity, and independent of the opinions of men, free of their partiality, of their hate and their malice, their power. It is *Al*mighty, for it is of God!

Unless you devote *all* your strength to severing yourselves from the old, you will not learn to comprehend this Justice either. But you will then likewise not be able to become new within! And only the *new* man, who stands in the Word of Life and strives towards the Light, will receive the help that he needs to pass through the Judgment of God.

Man must help himself through the Word, which shows him the ways he must follow! Only *thus* can he find redemption, otherwise it will not fall to his lot! He must grow strong in the battle that he wages for himself, or he must perish in it!

Awake, and present a fighting front to all Darkness, then you will also be given strength to help you. Weaklings, however, will lose even what strength they still possess, because they do not know how to use it properly. The little they have will thereby be taken away from them because, according to the Law of Attraction of Homogeneous Species, it flows to those who use this strength with zeal and in the *right manner.* Thus an ancient promise is fulfilled.

IT IS the sacred duty of the human spirit to investigate why it is living on earth, or in general in this Creation, in which it is suspended as if by a thousand threads. No man considers himself so insignificant as to imagine that his existence is without purpose, unless *he* makes it purposeless. In any case he deems himself too important. And yet there are only a few men on earth capable of laboriously detaching themselves from their spiritual indolence, *so* far as seriously to concern themselves with the investigation of their task on earth.

Again it is solely indolence of the spirit that makes them willing to accept the firmly-established doctrines of others. And it is indolence that lies in the reassurance that comes from thinking that it is great to adhere to the faith of their parents, without submitting its underlying principles to keen, careful and independent examination.

In all these matters men are now eagerly supported by calculating and selfish organisations, which believe that the best way to extend and safeguard their influence, and thus to increase their power, is by adding to the number of their adherents.

They are far from true recognition of God; for otherwise they would not bind the human spirit with the fetters of a firmly-established doctrine, but would have to educate it for the personal responsibility ordained by God, which fundamentally stipulates *full freedom of spiritual decision!* Only a spirit free in this respect can come to the true recognition of God that matures within him to the complete conviction which is essential for anyone who wishes to be uplifted to Luminous Heights; for only free, sincere conviction can help him to achieve this. –

But what have you done, you men! How have you suppressed this highest Grace of God and wantonly prevented it from developing, and from helping all earthmen to open up *that* path which safely leads them to peace, to joy, and to the highest bliss!

Consider this: that also in making a choice, in agreement or in obedience, which as a result of spiritual indolence may be done only from habit or general custom, a *personal decision is involved*, laying upon the individual who makes it personal responsibilities according to the Laws of Creation!

Those who influence a human spirit to do this naturally bear a personal responsibility, which is inevitable and irrevocable. No thought or action, however trivial, can be erased from Creation without similar consequences. In the web of Creation the threads both for the individual and for the masses are accurately spun, awaiting redemptions, which in turn must eventually be received by the originators or producers, either as suffering or as joy, according to how they once issued from them; only now they have grown and are thus strengthened.

You are caught in the web of your own volitions, of your actions, and are not released from it until the threads can fall away from you in the redemption.

Among all creatures in Creation the human spirit is the only one to have *free will*, which until today he could not explain and did not understand, because within the narrow bounds of his intellectual pondering he found no essential facts to prove it.

His free will lies solely in the *decision*, of which he may make many every hour. In the independent weaving of the Laws of Creation, however, he is unswervingly subject to the consequences of every one of his personal decisions! Therein lies his responsibility, which is inseparably connected with the gift of free will to make decisions, which is peculiar to and an absolute part of the human spirit.

Otherwise what would become of Divine Justice, which is firmly anchored in Creation as support, balance and maintenance of all the working therein?

In Its effects, however, It does not always take account of the short span of only one earth-life for a human spirit; but here there are entirely different conditions, as readers of my Message know.

You have often brought harm upon yourselves, and sometimes force it upon your children, through many superficial decisions. Even though you yourselves have proved too indolent still to summon up the strength to decide for yourselves in your deepest intuitive perception whether, regardless of all you have learnt, each word to which you decided to adhere can hold Truth, at least you should not seek to force the consequences of your indolence also upon your children, whom you thus plunge into misfortune.

Thus what in one case is caused by spiritual indolence, in others is brought about by the calculating intellect.

Through both these enemies of spiritual freedom in decision mankind is now bound, except for a few who still try to summon up the courage to burst this bond within them in order to become real human beings themselves, as follows from obedience to the Divine Laws.

The Divine Laws are true friends in everything, they are helpful blessings from the Will of God, Who thus opens the paths to salvation for everyone who strives towards it.

There is not a single other road to this than the one clearly shown by the Laws of God in Creation! The whole of Creation is the Language of God, which you should earnestly strive to read, and which is by no means as difficult as you may think.

You belong to this Creation as a part of it, and therefore you must swing with it, work in it, and mature in learning from it; and thus through gaining in understanding you must rise ever higher, from one step to the next, drawing along through the radiation in order to ennoble everything that comes in contact with you on your way.

There will then spontaneously develop around you one beautiful miracle after another, which through reciprocal action will raise you ever higher.

Learn to recognise your path in Creation, and you will also know the purpose of your existence. Then you will be filled with grateful rejoicing, and the greatest happiness a human spirit is able to bear, which lies solely in the recognition of God!

The supreme bliss of the true recognition of God, however, can never grow out of an acquired blind faith, much less come to flower; but convinced knowledge, knowing conviction, alone gives to the spirit what is necessary for this.

You earthmen are in this Creation to *find* supreme happiness! In the Living Language which God speaks to you! And to understand this Language, to learn it, and to sense inwardly the Will of God in it, *that* is your *goal* during your journey through Creation. In Creation itself, to which you belong, lies the explanation of the *purpose* of your existence, and at the same time also the recognition of your *goal!* In no other way can you find either.

This demands of you that you *live* Creation. But you are only able to live or *experience* it when you really *know* it.

With my Message I now open the Book of Creation for you! The Message clearly shows you the Language of God in Creation, which you must learn to understand so that you can make it completely your own.

Just imagine a child on earth who cannot understand his father or mother because he has never learned the language they speak to him. Indeed, what is to become of such a child?

He does not even know what is expected of him, and will thus fall into one difficulty after the other, draw upon himself one sorrow after another, and probably end up utterly useless for any purpose or enjoyment on earth.

If he is to amount to anything, must not every child *personally* learn the language of his parents for himself? Nobody can do it for him!

Otherwise he would never adjust himself, nor would he ever be able to mature and work on earth, but he would remain a hindrance, a burden to others, and would finally have to be segregated to prevent him from causing harm.

Could you expect anything else then?

You have of course inescapably to fulfil such a duty of the child towards your God, Whose Language *you* must learn to understand as soon as you desire His help. God, however, speaks to you in His Creation. If you want to advance in it, you must first recognise this His Language. Should you neglect it, you will be cut off from those who know the Language and adjust themselves to it, because you would otherwise cause harm and obstruction, without necessarily wishing to do so!

You must therefore do it! Do not forget this, and see that it is done now, otherwise you will be helplessly abandoned to whatever threatens you.

My Message will be a faithful helper to you!

ALPHABETICAL INDEX

CONTENTS
OF VOLUMES II AND III OF THIS WORK

VOLUME II

VOLUME III

ABD-RU-SHIN
AUTHOR OF THE GRAIL MESSAGE

His civil name is Oskar Ernst Bernhardt. He was born in Bischofswerda, Saxony, on 18th April 1875.

In 1919 he became conscious of his task to open the way for a new Knowledge of Creation. For this purpose he chose the name Abd-ru-shin.

In the years 1923 to 1937 there came into being those lectures which were later combined and published by him in the Work "In the Light of Truth" The Grail Message.

He did not compile his Message from other teachings of ancient and modern times, but drew his Living Knowledge from the purest and highest Source, thus creating his Message from the Grail, which indeed is his actual identity!

Like every Truth-bringer he too was hindered in his beneficial working. Abd-ru-shin died on 6th December 1941. But his Work lives on, and works to help all men who are earnestly seeking the Truth.

"In the Light of Truth"
The Grail Message
by Abd-ru-shin

Edition in three volumes

Pocket edition in three volumes

Original edition: German

Translations available in:
Czech, Dutch, English, French, Italian,
Portuguese, Russian, Spanish

Prices available on request.

FURTHER WRITINGS BY ABD-RU-SHIN

The Ten Commandments of God and The Lord's Prayer
Explained to mankind by Abd-ru-shin.
72 pages, paperback.

Questions and Answers
Answers by Abd-ru-shin to questions with which he was
approached during the years 1924-1937.
232 pages, paperback.

Prayers
Given to mankind by Abd-ru-shin.
16 pages, staple-bound.

DISTRIBUTED IN:

AMERICA: GRAIL FOUNDATION OF AMERICA
14318 Shirley Bohn Road, Mt. Airy, MD 21711, USA
Tel: +1 607 723 5163
e-mail: info@grailmessage.com

AUSTRALIA: GRAIL MOVEMENT IN AUSTRALIA
13 Bareena Drive, Mt Eliza, VIC 3930, Australia
Tel: +61 3 9005 774
e-mail: contact@grail.org.au

CANADA: GRAIL MOVEMENT IN CANADA
C.P. 3568, Chénéville, QC J0V 1E0, Canada
Tel: +1 819 428 7001, +1 877 762 3077
e-mail: info@grailmovement.ca

GREAT BRITAIN: GRAIL MOVEMENT IN THE UK & IRELAND
Suite F6, Flemington House, 110 Flemington Street
Glasgow, Scotland, G21 4BF, Great Britain
Tel: +44 141 558 7133
e-mail: info@grailmovement-uk.org

NEW ZEALAND: GRAIL MOVEMENT IN NEW ZEALAND
P.O. Box 32-006, Devonport, North Shore
Auckland 0744, New Zealand
Tel & Fax: +64 9 4451707
e-mail: info@grailmovement.org.nz

AFRICA: GRAIL MOVEMENT IN NIGERIA
Plot 22, Block 96, Babatunde Dabiri Street
Lekki Phase I, Lekki, Lagos
Tel: +234 1 471 324; +234 1 810 4699; +234 1 791 4991
e-mail: info@grailmovement-nigeria.org

Or visit us on internet: www.grail-message.com